WORLD ENGLISH 1

THIRD EDITION

Real People • Real Places • Real Language

John Hughes, Author

Martin Milner, Author

NATIONAL GEOGRAPHIC

LEARNING

Australia • Brazil • Mexico • Singapore • United Kingdom • United States

National Geographic Learning,
a Cengage Company

World English Level 1: Real People, Real Places, Real Language, Third Edition
John Hughes and Martin Milner

Publisher: Sherrise Roehr

Executive Editor: Sarah Kenney

Senior Development Editor: Brenden Layte

Media Researcher: Leila Hishmeh

Senior Technology Product Manager:
  Lauren Krolick

Director of Global Marketing: Ian Martin

Senior Product Marketing Manager:
  Caitlin Thomas

Heads of Regional Marketing:
  Charlotte Ellis (Europe, Middle East, and Africa)
  Kiel Hamm (Asia)
  Irina Pereyra (Latin America)

Production Manager: Daisy Sosa

Manufacturing Planner: Mary Beth Hennebury

Art Director: Brenda Carmichael

Operations Support: Hayley Chwazik-Gee

Cover Image: Trey Ratcliff

Compositor: MPS Limited

World English 1 ISBN: 978-0-357-11368-4
World English 1 + MyWorldEnglishOnline ISBN: 978-0-357-13020-9

National Geographic Learning
200 Pier 4 Boulevard
Boston, MA 02210
USA

Locate your local office at **international.cengage.com/region**

Visit National Geographic Learning online at **ELTNGL.com**
Visit our corporate website at www.cengage.com

Printed in Singapore
Print Number: 01 Print Year: 2022

Thank you to the educators who provided invaluable feedback during the development of the third edition of the *World English* series:

AMERICAS

Brazil

Gabriely Billordo, Berlitz, Porto Alegre
Bruna Caltabiano, Caltabiano Idiomas, Sao Paulo
Sophia de Carvalho, Inglês Express, Belo Horizonte
Renata Coelho, 2b English for you, Florianopolis
Rebecca Ashley Hibas, Inglês Express, Belo Horizonte
Cristina Kobashi, Cultivar Escola de Idiomas, Guaratinguetá
Silvia Teles Barbosa, Colégio Cândido Portinari, Salvador

Chile

Jorge Cuevas, Universidad Santo Tomás, Los Angeles

Colombia

Ruben Cano, UPB University, Medellin
Javier Vega, Fundación Universitaria de Popayán, Popayán

Costa Rica

Jonathan Acuña, Centro Cultural Costarricense Americano, San José
Lilly Sevilla, Centro Cultural Costarricense Americano, San José

Mexico

José Aguirre, Instituto Tecnológico Superior de Irapuato, Salamanca
Alejandro Alvarado Cupil, Instituto Tecnológico de Minatitlán, Minatitlán
Jhosellin Ángeles, ITSOEH, Mixquiahuala de Juárez, Hidalgo
René Bautista, BUAP, Puebla
Imelda Félix, Colegio Cervantes Costa Rica, Guadalajara
Isabel Fernández, Universidad Autónoma de Aguascalientes, Aguascalientes
Andrés Garcia, FES Aragón (UNAM), Mexico City
Jéssica Garcia, Colegio Cultural, Puebla
Lázaro Garcia, Tecnológico de Toluca, Metepec
Fernando Gómez, Universidad Tecnológica Jalisco,Guadalajara
Alma Gopar, FES Zaragoza (UNAM), Mexico City
Inés Gutiérrez, University of Colima, Colima
Jesús Chávez Hernández, Universidad Aeronáutica en Querétaro, Colón
Cristina Méndez, Instituto Tecnológico Superior de Irapuato, Irapuato
Elena Mioto, UNIVA, Guadalajara
Rubén Mauricio Muñoz Morales, Universidad Santo Tomás, Villavicencio
María Rodríguez, Universidad Aeronáutica en Querétaro, Colón
Ana Lilia Terrazas, ICO, Puebla

United States

Amy Fouts, Face to Face Learning Center, Doral, FL
Virginia Jorge, UCEDA International, New Brunswick, NJ
Richard McDorman, Language On, Miami, FL
Sarah Mikulski, Harper College, Palatine, IL
Rachel Scheiner, Seattle Central College, Seattle, WA
Pamela Smart-Smith, Virginia Tech Language and Culture Institute, Blacksburg, VA
Marcie Stone, American English College, Rowland Heights, CA
Colin Ward, Lone Star College-North Harris, Houston, TX
Marla Yoshida, University California Irvine, CA

ASIA

Nazarul Azali, UiTM Cawangan Melaka, Alor Gajah
Steven Bretherick, Tohoku Fukushi University, Sendai
Sam Bruce, Soka University, Hachioji
Karen Cline-Katayama, Hokusei Gakuen University and Tokai University, Sapporo
Tom David, Japan College of Foreign Languages, Tokyo
Johnny Eckstein, Soka University, Hachioji
Meg Ellis, Kyoto Tachibana University, Kyoto
Thomas Goetz, Hokusei Gakuen University, Sapporo
Katsuko Hirai, Matsuyama University, Matsuyama
Paul Horness, Soka University, Hachioji
David Kluge, Nanzan University, Nagoya
Stephen Lambacher, Aoyama Gakuin University, Tokyo
Yi-An Lin, National Taipei University of Business, Taipei
Kerry McCatty, Soka University, Hachioji
Gregg McNabb, Shizuoka Institute of Technology, Shizuoka
Collin Mehmet, Matsumoto University, Matsumoto City
Sean Mehmet, Shinshu University, Matsumoto
Lin Mingying, Soka University, Hachioji
Erika Nakatsuka, Soka University, Hachioji
Seiko Oguri, Chubu University, Nagoya
Thomas Nishikawa, Ritsumeikan University, Kyoto
Sean Otani, Tottori University, Tottori
Daniel Paller, Kinjo Gakuin University, Nagoya
Tomomi Sasaki, Ibaraki University, Mito
Mark Shrosbree, Tokai University, Hiratsuka
Brent Simmons, Aichi Gakuin University, Nagoya
Mikiko Sudo, Soka University, Hachioji
Monika Szirmai, Hiroshima International University, Hiroshima
Matthew Taylor, Kinjo Gakuin University, Nagoya
James Thomas, Kokusai Junior College, Tokyo
Asca Tsushima, Soka University, Hachioji
Hui Chun Yu, Macau University of Science and Technology, Macau

Listening	Speaking and Pronunciation	Reading	Writing	Video Journal
Focused Listening: An Interview, Personal Introductions	Asking For and Giving Personal Information Starting a Conversation Contractions of *be* Word Stress	The Best Job in the World	Writing Descriptions of People Using Conjunctions	**Where I Am a Local** In this video from National Geographic Learning, author Taiye Selasi talks about who she is, the places she comes from, and what it means to be a local somewhere.
Focused Listening: A Radio Show about an Astronaut's Daily Life	Talking about Daily Schedules and Free Time Showing Interest Verbs that end in *-s*	When Your Hobby is Also Your Job	Writing an Email to Make Plans Parts of an Email	**Ruben's Elevator** This film, from the National Geographic Short Film Showcase, gives a glimpse into the life of Ruben Pardo, the oldest manual elevator operator in Los Angeles, California.
General Listening: Conversations During Stages of Travel	Identifying Possession of Items Giving Personal Information for Travel Forms Asking for and Giving Advice Rising and Falling Intonation	Make Your Vacation More Interesting	Writing a Description of a Place Conjunctions: *because, so*	**The UK in 100 Seconds** In this film, National Geographic Explorer Daniel Raven-Ellison gives a look at the landscapes that make up the UK, and offers suggestions for how the use of land can be improved.
General and Focused Listening: Ordering a Meal in a Restaurant	Role-play: Ordering a Meal Talking about Quantities Reduced Forms: *Do you have...* and *Would you like...*	Urban Farming	Giving Instructions Sequencing Information	**A Guerrilla Gardener in South Central LA** In this TED Talk, Ron Finley talks about LA Green Grounds, an organization he founded to show people in his neighborhood how to live a healthy and sustainable life that gives back to the community.
General and Focused Listening: Phone Calls about Everyday Activities and Today's Activities	Talking about What People are Doing Now Discussing Favorite Sports Talking about Likes and Dislikes Reduced Form: *What are you ...*	eSports Go Global	Writing and Completing a Questionnaire Closed and Open Questions	**Free Soloing with Alex Honnold** In this video from National Geographic, climber and National Geographic Explorer Alex Honnold takes you up the massive Half Dome rock formation in Yosemite National Park in California ... without a rope!
General Listening: Conversations about Vacations and Weekend Trips	Describing and Comparing Vacations Asking about Your Weekend Discuss Where You Find Information Sounds of *-ed* Endings	The Cradle of the Inca Empire	Writing an Online Post Using Time References	**Vietnam's Green Jewels** This video from National Geographic gives information about the history and background of one of the world's most beautiful places: Vietnam's Ha Long Bay.

Listening	Speaking and Pronunciation	Reading	Writing	Video Journal
Focused Listening: Exchanging Contact Information via a Voicemail, a Radio Call-In Show, and a Conversation	Asking for Contact Information Describing Sights, Sounds, and Other Sensations Giving Your Opinion Sentence Stress for Clarification	Do You Speak "Elephant"?	Writing Emails Asking for Information and Making Plans Formal and Informal Writing	**A New View of the Moon** In this video from National Geographic's Short Film Showcase, filmmaker Wylie Overstreet takes a telescope to the city streets and asks people to look up and see the moon in a new way.
General and Focused Listening: An Interview with National Geographic Explorer Molly Ferrill about Her Latest Project	Talking about Short- and Long-Term Plans Making Predictions and Giving Opinions about the Future Discussing a Personality Quiz Reduced form of *going to*	Electricity from the Sun	Analyzing Graphs to Describe Trends Describing Trends	**A Virtual Choir 2,000 Voices Strong** In this TED Talk, composer Eric Whitacre talks about the virtual choir, a group of singers from around the world who come together online to make music and share their stories.
Focused Listening: A Conversation between a Shopper and Assistant in a Shoe Store	Talking about Clothes Role-Play Different Shopping Experiences Stressed and Weak Syllables	Pride through Fashion	Writing an Ad that Describes Clothes Describing Objects Adjective Order Punctuation	**How Your T-Shirt Can Make a Difference** In this video from National Geographic, the goods and resources that are used to make a T-shirt are shown, and a question is asked: How can your shopping and clothing care decisions make a difference?
General Listening: Personal Descriptions of Lifestyles and Habits	Discussing Healthy and Unhealthy Habits Asking and Telling about Lifestyles Approximation *Have to*	The Need for Sleep	Writing a Paragraph about a Healthy Hobby or Activity Paragraph Structure	**Living Past 100** In this video from National Geographic, the region of Bama, China, is profiled. It is one of the healthiest and most beautiful parts of the country.
Listening for General Understanding and Specific Details: Job Interviews for a Tour Guide Position	Interviewing for a Job Catching Up with a Friend Using Present Perfect and Simple Past in Conversations Reduced Forms of *have*	Being the First in Less than Two Hours	Writing a Resume Checking for Mistakes in Writing	**Wasfia's Journey** In this video from National Geographic's Short Film Showcase, mountain climber, activist, and National Geographic Explorer Wasfia Nazreen talks about climbing the tallest mountain on each of the seven continents, and what her journey means to the people of her country.
Listening for Specific Details and Key Information: A Podcast about a Trip that Didn't Waste Plastic	Discuss How to Save Money Talking about Choices Conditional Intonation	Crowdfunding for a Better World	Write an Email about a Major Decision Compare and Contrast	**How to Buy Happiness** In this video from National Geographic Learning, social scientist Michael Norton talks about the ways that money can, and can't, affect our well-being and that of those around us.

People

Look at the photo and answer the questions.

1 Who are these people? Are they happy?

2 How are you today? Are you happy?

Two friends take a selfie at a concert in Pula, Croatia.

UNIT 1 GOALS

A. Meet People

B. Ask for Personal Information

C. Describe People and Occupations

D. Compare People's Jobs

E. Write a Personal Description

GOAL Meet People

Vocabulary

A Fill in the blanks. Use the map and the words in the box.

chef	dancer	journalist	musician	photographer
pilot	police officer	student	teacher	travel agent

1. This is Norma. She's from _____Mexico_____ and she's a _____dancer_____.
2. This is Gabriela. She's from _____ and she's a _____.
3. This is Frank. He's from _____ and he's a _____.
4. This is Marie. She's from _____ and she's a _____.
5. This is Yaseen. He's from _____ and he's a _____.
6. This is Luis. He's from _____ and he's a _____.
7. This is Kaya. She's from _____ and she's a _____.
8. This is Cho. He's from _____ and he's a _____.
9. This is Nanako. She's from _____ and she's a _____.
10. This is Nicolas. He's from _____ and he's a _____.

REAL LANGUAGE

We say **What does she / he do?** to ask about a person's occupation or job.

B In pairs, talk about the people in the photos.

> Where is Norma from?

> Norma is from Mexico.

> What does she do?

> She's a dancer.

4 Unit 1

Grammar: *Be*

Affirmative			Negative		
I	**am / 'm**	a student.	I	**am not / 'm not**	a student.
You / We / They	**are / 're**	from Mexico.	You / We / They	**are not / aren't**	from Mexico.
He / She / It	**is / 's**	a dancer.	He / She / It	**is not / isn't**	a dancer.

C Match the question to the answer.

1. Are you a doctor? _____

2. Is she from China? _____

3. Is Ben from London? _____

4. Are Mario and Teresa students? _____

Yes / *No* Questions			Short Answers
Are	you / they	Mexican?	Yes, I **am**. / No, I**'m** not.
Is	he / she / it		Yes, they **are**. / No, they **aren't**.
			Yes, he **is**. / No, he **isn't**.

   a. Yes, he is.   **c.** Yes, they are.

   b. No, she isn't.   **d.** No, I'm not. I'm a nurse.

D 🎧 **2** Complete the conversation with the correct form of *be*. Listen and check.

Sean: Hi, my name's Sean.

Claudia: Nice to meet you, Sean. I (1) _____'m____ Claudia, from Chile.

Sean: (2) _____ you from Santiago?

Claudia: Yes, I (3) _____. And you? Where are you from?

Sean: I'm from Toronto, in Canada, but I (4) _____ a student here.

Claudia: I'm in New York for two weeks. My brother (5) _____ a student at NYU.

Sean: (6) _____ he here?

Claudia: No, he (7) _____. Are you here with friends?

Sean: Yes, I am. We (8) _____ at that table. Come and meet them! This is Claudia. She (9) _____ from Chile. This is Maria and Nico. They (10) _____ also students at NYU.

REAL LANGUAGE

Say **Nice to meet you** when you meet someone for the first time.

E Practice the conversation in pairs. Switch roles and practice it again.

Pronunciation: Contractions of *Be*

F 🎧 **3** Listen. Circle the full form or the contraction. Listen again and repeat.

1. *I am /* (*I'm*) *Claudia.*

2. *He is / He's from New York.*

3. *She is not / She isn't a teacher.*

4. *They are / They're students.*

5. *We are not / We aren't from the US.*

6. *You are / You're from Santiago.*

 GOAL CHECK Meet People

1. Choose a new name, country, and occupation for yourself. Then introduce yourself to another student.

2. Introduce your partner to another pair.

> Hello. My name is Jason. I'm from China.

B GOAL Ask for Personal Information

Listening

A Look at the photos. Guess the missing information with a partner.

B 🎧 4 Listen to four interviews. Complete the profiles.

1. Name: Kyoko Hashimoto

Nationality: _____

City: Tokyo

Country: Japan

Occupation: _____

3. Name: Jim Waters

Nationality: _____

City: Stratford

Country: _____

Occupation: Farmer

2. Name: Luis Gomez

Nationality: _____

City: Lima

Country: _____

Occupation: _____

4. Name: Bianca da Silva

Nationality: _____

City: Rio de Janeiro

Country: _____

Occupation: Musician

WORD FOCUS

Sometimes we add suffixes to words to make occupations and nationalities:
journal → journal**ist**
music → music**ian**
science → scient**ist**
teach → teach**er**
Australia → Australi**an**
Chile → Chile**an**
China → Chin**ese**
England → Engl**ish**
Ireland → Ir**ish**
Japan → Japan**ese**
Mexico → Mexic**an**

Vocabulary

C Write the countries and nationalities to complete the chart.

Countries	Nationalities
Canada	1. _Canadian_
2. _____	Chinese
3. _____	Australian
Mexico	4. _____
5. _____	Japanese
Ireland	6. _____

Pronunciation: Word Stress

D 🎧 5 Listen to the countries and nationalities in the chart. Underline the stressed syllables. Then listen again and repeat.

E In pairs, look back at the people in the map on page 4. Say new sentences about each person's nationality.

> Norma is Mexican.

F MY WORLD How many nationalities are in your family? Is everyone from the same country, or from different countries?

Grammar

Wh- Questions with *Be*		
Wh- word	*be*	
What **Where** **Who** **How old**	**is** **are**	your name? / his nationality? / their occupation? you from? / she from? / they from? your teacher? / your friends? you? / she? / they?

G Make *Wh-* questions for these answers.

1. I'm from South Korea. _Where are you from?_ _____

2. My English teachers are Mr. Samuel and Mrs. Gomez. _____

3. Her name is Karina Lopez. _____

4. She's 32 years old. _____

5. They're Canadian. _____

H In pairs, ask for personal information. Ask and answer five *Wh-* questions.

> What's your name?

I Work in pairs. Student A chooses a card below. Student B asks *Yes / No* and *Wh-* questions to find out which card Student A has.

> How old are you?

B: How old are you? **A:** 28 years old.

B: Are you a pilot? **A:** No, I'm not.

B: What's your nationality? **A:** Argentinian.

B: Is your name Pablo? **A:** Yes, it is!

Name: Andrew Nationality: American Age: 28 Job: Pilot	Name: Mi Hi Nationality: Korean Age: 23 Job: Architect	Name: Kwan Nationality: Korean Age: 30 Job: Architect
Name: Pablo Nationality: Argentinian Age: 28 Job: Doctor	Name: Helen Nationality: American Age: 30 Job: Doctor	Name: Ana Nationality: Argentinian Age: 23 Job: Teacher

 GOAL CHECK
Ask for Personal Information

Play "Who am I?" in small groups. One student chooses a famous person. The others ask for personal information. You can ask 10 *Yes / No* or *Wh-* questions. Try to guess the person without asking for the name!

> What's your nationality?

> Are you a man?

> How old are you?

> Are you a musician?

GOAL Describe People and Occupations

Language Expansion: Describing People and Occupations

easy

sad

boring

rich

dangerous

difficult

happy

interesting

poor

safe

A Write the adjectives in the correct column.

Affirmative	Negative
happy,	sad,

B Which adjectives normally describe:

- people? happy,
- occupations? easy,
- both? interesting,

C Read the sentences. Circle the adjective that you agree with. Compare your answers with a partner. Discuss any differences.

1. Dan is a travel agent. His job is *interesting / boring*.
2. Gabriela is a police officer. Her job is *safe / dangerous*.
3. Mario's job does not pay a high salary. He is *happy / unhappy*.
4. Ismael is a doctor. He is *rich / poor*.
5. Yuki is a teacher. Her job is *easy / difficult*.

D In pairs, use adjectives to describe the people on page 4.

WORD FOCUS

salary money earned through work

Grammar

Subject	*Be*	Adjective
You	**are**	happy.
My job	**is**	interesting.

Subject	*Be*		Adjective	Noun
You	**are**	a	happy	person.
It	**is**	an	interesting	job.

E Unscramble the words to make sentences.

1. job / friend's / is / My / dangerous. _____

2. is / person. / interesting / Kim's / friend / an _____

3. your / happy? / brother / Is _____

4. rich / is / not / a / My / father / man. _____

F Complete the sentences so they are true for you. Share your answers with a partner.

1. My best friend is _____.

2. My job is _____.

3. _____ is an interesting person.

4. _____ is boring.

SPEAKING STRATEGY

Starting a Conversation
Nice to meet you.
 Nice to meet you, too.
Where are you from?
 I'm from (the US).
What do you do?
 I'm (an engineer).
What's your job like?
 It's (interesting).
Is it (exciting)?
 Sometimes it's (boring).

Conversation

G 🎧 6 Two people meet for the first time. Listen and fill in the table.

	What are their jobs?	What adjectives describe the jobs?
Elsa	engineer	
Graham		

H 🎧 6 Listen again and read the conversation. Then practice the conversation with a partner. Switch roles and practice it again.

Graham: Hi, my name's Graham. Nice to meet you.

Elsa: Nice to meet you, too. I'm Elsa.

Graham: What do you do, Elsa?

Elsa: I'm an engineer.

Graham: An engineer. That's an interesting job!

Elsa: Yes, it is, but it's difficult sometimes. What do you do?

Graham: I'm a forest ranger.

Elsa: Really? What's that like? Is it exciting?

Graham: Yes, most of the time, but sometimes it's boring. Just me and the trees!

A forest ranger is at a waterfall in Aceh, Indonesia.

✓ **GOAL CHECK**
Describe People and Occupations

Think of a new name and occupation for yourself. Then work with a partner and start a new conversation.

• Introduce yourself.

• Ask about your partner's occupation.

• Describe your occupation.

D GOAL Compare People's Jobs

Reading

A Look at the photos. What do you think the people in the article do?

B Read the article. Circle **T** for *true* and **F** for *false*.

1. A job with a good salary is always interesting.   **T   F**
2. Animals are not easy to photograph.   **T   F**
3. Jeff says his job is boring.   **T   F**
4. Maritza is from Mexico.   **T   F**
5. There are tables and chairs in her classroom.   **T   F**
6. Ross and Marty work in one place.   **T   F**
7. They like Patagonia because every day is different.   **T   F**

C Answer the questions.

1. What does Jeff do?
   _____

2. Do you think Jeff is happy?
   _____

3. Where is Maritza's classroom?
   _____

4. What are her lessons about?
   _____

5. What do Ross and Marty do?
   _____

6. Where is Patagonia?
   _____

D Complete the chart. Write one job in each box.

	Good salary	Bad salary
Interesting		
Boring		
Difficult		
Easy		

✓ GOAL CHECK

In pairs, compare your answers in **D**. Then discuss which job on your lists is the best. Why?

The Best Job in the World

What is a good job? Is it a job with a good salary? Not always. For some people, their salary is good, but their job is boring. And for other people, their salary isn't good, but the job is easy. And some people are happy because their jobs are interesting. Let's meet some people with great jobs.

Maritza Morales Casanova is Mexican and she's from Merida. She's a teacher, but there are

no tables or chairs in her classroom because it's a park. The children learn about nature in the park. She says, "**Empower** children with information… and they will change the world."

Jeff Kerby is a National Geographic photographer. Animals are difficult to photograph, so the job isn't easy. Sometimes, the job is very difficult, but when you have a bad day, you look at the beautiful views and, Jeff says, "life isn't so bad, in fact, it's really interesting."

Ross Donihue and **Marty Schnure** are mapmakers. For their job, they travel and they

make **digital** maps of different parts of the world. One of their favorite places is Patagonia, in Argentina. Ross says, "I love Patagonia because no two days are the same. Every day is different."

empower give control to
digital electronic

This photo of a bleeding heart monkey is by Jeff Kerby.

GOAL Write a Personal Description

Communication

A Read the ad for college jobs. Answer the questions.

    1. When are the jobs for? _____

    2. Who is the ad for? _____

    3. What are the three jobs? _____

> ### ARE YOU A STUDENT?
> There are jobs for you in July and August!
> – Summer school assistants: Play sports and games with children
> – Waiters at a pizza restaurant: At lunchtime and in the evening
> – Cashier in a supermarket: The pay is good!
> Email: info@summerjobs.com

B Work with a partner. Which adjectives describe the three jobs? Use words from the unit or others you know.

C Which summer job is good for you? Why? Tell your partner.

> This job is good because...   ... it's interesting.   ... I like children.   ... it's easy.

D Read about three students in Toronto, Canada. Complete the notes in this table.

Name	Age	Home Country	Type of Student
Tanya	20		
Mateo		Colombia	
Aya			Tourism

Tanya Hello. My name's Tanya and I'm 20 years old. I'm from Australia, but I'm in Toronto now. I'm a business student.

Mateo Hi. I'm Mateo Gomez and I'm 23 years old. I'm from Colombia. In Bogota, I'm a teacher, but this year I'm a student in Toronto. I study English because I want to teach it back home.

Aya My name's Aya. Most of my family is Japanese, but I'm from Singapore. I'm 20 years old and I'm a tourism student.

E Which job in **A** is good for each of the students in **D**? Talk about the students with your partner.

> Summer school assistant is good for...because he / she...

Writing

WRITING SKILL: Using Conjunctions

When you use short sentences all the time (e.g., *I'm from Australia. I'm 20 years old.*), your writing isn't interesting. Writing is better with conjunctions (*and, but*) that connect short sentences to make longer ones.

F Compare the sentences. Then complete the rules with *and* and *but*.

My name's Tanya. I'm 20 years old.   *I'm from Australia. I'm in Toronto now.*
*My name's Tanya **and** I'm 20 years old.* *I'm from Australia, **but** I'm in Toronto now.*

1. _____ is for extra information.   2. _____ is for different information.

G Underline *and* and *but* in the personal information in **D**.

H Complete the sentences with *and* or *but*.

1. Angeline is from Brazil _____ she's 18 years old.

2. Asef is a student in England, _____ he's from Jordan.

3. I'm 35 years old _____ I'm a photographer.

4. My mother is Spanish, _____ my father isn't. He's Chinese.

5. She's 21 _____ I'm 21, too.

 GOAL CHECK Write a Personal Description

Write a personal description with *and* and *but*. Write about your:

- name.   • country.   • age.   • occupation.

Include other interesting information. Then share your descriptions in small groups.

Hi, I'm Andrés Ruzo. I'm from Peru, but I live in the US. I'm a scientist and a National Geographic Explorer.

A Answer the questions.

1. Where are you from? ▭
2. Where do you live now? ▭
3. Where do you feel at home? ▭

B Watch the interviews. Where are the people from?

1. ▭
2. ▭
3. ▭
4. ▭

C Where do the people feel at home? Complete the quotes from the video.

1. I live in ▭ .
2. I speak ▭ a little bit, Russian, Portuguese, and ▭ .
3. I would say right now ▭ is my home.
4. I identify myself as from ▭ , not from a single city.

D Watch the rest of the video. Circle **T** for *true* or **F** for *false*.

1. Taiye says that "Where are you from?" is a difficult question. **T** **F**
2. Taiye's parents live in Ghana. **T** **F**
3. Taiye lived in the UK for a long time. **T** **F**
4. Taiye lives in the US. **T** **F**
5. The question "Where are you a local?" is about people, not places. **T** **F**
6. Taiye is a local in Lisbon. **T** **F**
7. A place is local if people you love are there. **T** **F**
8. You can only be a local in one country. **T** **F**

E MY WORLD Think about the question *Where are you a local?* Is it an easy or difficult question for you to answer? Why?

F Prepare a two-minute presentation about yourself called *Where I am a local*. Present your talk to the class or make a video to share with the class. You can use your notes from **A** and some of these phrases:

Hello. My name is…

My presentation is about the question "Where are you from?"

For me, it's an easy / difficult question.

I'm… years old and I'm a…

I was born in…

My parents are from…

I live in… I study…

So the question "Where are you a local?" is an easy / difficult question for me.

Taiye Selasi, Author

A Day in the Life

Crab fishermen have a dangerous job, but still have fun. They work on boats and catch crabs.

Look at the photo and answer the questions.

1 Where are these men? Do they like their job?

2 When do you work? When do you have free time?

UNIT 2 GOALS

A. Talk about a Typical Day

B. Talk about Free Time

C. Describe a Special Day

D. Talk about Hobbies and Interests

E. Plan a Party

17

GOAL Talk about a Typical Day

Vocabulary

brush your teeth
catch the bus
drink coffee
eat breakfast
get up
go to bed
go to class / a
  meeting
have lunch
leave school
start work
take a break
take a shower

A Label the pictures. Use the phrases in the box.

1. _____

2. _____

3. _____

4. _____

5. _____

6. _____

7. _____

8. _____

9. _____

10. _____

11. _____

12. _____

WORD FOCUS

We often use
these verb + noun
collocations when
we talk about daily
routines:

*eat / have breakfast /
lunch / dinner*

*drink / have coffee /
tea*

*catch the bus / train /
subway*

start work / school

B Circle the activities in **A** that you do every day.

C In your notebook, write the activities from **A** in the order that you do them.

D Describe your order from **C** to a partner. Use *first, next, then,* and *finally*.

First I get up, and
then I take a shower
and brush my teeth.

Grammar

Simple Present		
Statements		
I / You / We / They	**start** **don't start**	work at nine o'clock.
He / She / It	**starts** **doesn't start**	
Questions	**Short Answers**	
Do you **start** work at nine o'clock? **Does** she **start** work at nine o'clock? What time **do** you **get up**? What time **does** she **start** work?	Yes, I **do**. / No, I **don't**. Yes, she **does**. / No, she **doesn't**. At seven o'clock. At nine o'clock.	

E 🎧 8   Complete the questions and answers. Then listen and check.

Omar: So, Mia, what time (1) _____ you _____ work?

Mia: I start work at nine o'clock.

Omar: (2) _____ you finish work at five, then?

Mia: No, I (3) _____. I finish at six.

Omar: That's a long day! What time (4) _____ you eat dinner?

Mia: My family (5) _____ dinner at eight. Then we (6) _____ to bed at ten.

F   Practice the conversation in pairs. Switch roles and practice it again.

G   Write information about your typical day in the **You** column (for example, *7 a.m.: get up*). Include at least two activities for each time of day.

	You	Your Partner
In the Morning		
In the Afternoon		
In the Evening		

 GOAL CHECK Talk about a Typical Day

In pairs, ask questions and talk about your typical day. Write information about your partner in the table in **G**.

> What time do you get up?

> At 7 o'clock. Then I eat breakfast at 8.

GOAL Talk about Free Time

Listening

A What do you do in your free time? Check (✓) the activities on the list.

- ☐ watch TV
- ☐ get exercise (e.g., go running)
- ☐ read books
- ☐ play games
- ☐ take photographs
- ☐ go to the movies
- ☐ play a musical instrument (e.g., piano, guitar)
- ☐ eat out

B 🎧 9 Listen to a radio show about Drew Feustal. Drew is an astronaut on the International Space Station. Which activities in **A** does Drew do in his free time?

C 🎧 9 Listen again. Circle the correct answer.

1. The astronauts always get up at _____.

   a. six o'clock   **b.** seven o'clock   **c.** eight o'clock

2. Drew starts work _____.

   a. at nine o'clock   **b.** after he does exercise   **c.** after breakfast

3. When does he take photographs?

   a. at night   **b.** in the afternoon   **c.** on weekends

4. When do they have free time on the weekends?

   a. All day Saturday and Sunday

   b. Saturday afternoon and Sunday

   c. Saturday and Sunday mornings

WORD FOCUS

We often talk about our free time with **go**:

go to (a place or event): *go to the movies / park / football game*

go + *-ing* (an activity): *go running / shopping / swimming*

D 🎧 10 Listen and check (✓) the correct row.

PRONUNCIATION: Verbs that End in -s	starts	comes	catches	watches	gets	eats	goes
Ends with /s/							
Ends with /z/							
Ends with /ɪz/							

Drew Feustal works on the International Space Station.

E [10] Listen again. Repeat the words.

F Write sentences in your notebook about what you do in your free time. Use the activities in **A**. In pairs, read each other's sentences aloud and check each other's pronunciation.

Communication

G Use the words to write questions.

1. you / go to the movies / Saturdays _Do you go to the movies on Saturdays?_

2. you / get up / eight o'clock / weekends _____

3. you / watch TV / Sunday mornings _____

4. you / get exercise / evening _____

5. you / eat out / weekends _____

H Interview two classmates. Use the questions in **G** and your own ideas. Write *yes* or *no*.

	Classmate 1	Classmate 2
1. Name?		
2. go to the movies?		
3. get up?		
4. watch TV?		
5. get exercise?		
6. eat out?		
7. _____?		
8. _____?		

 GOAL CHECK Talk about Free Time

Tell a partner about the interviews in **H**.

Ana goes to the movies on Saturdays, and so does Sebastian.

Ana goes to the movies on Saturdays, but Lin doesn't.

Ahmet doesn't watch TV on Saturdays, but Sebastian does.

Ahmet doesn't go to the movies on Saturdays, and neither does Lin.

WORD FOCUS

Use **so do / does** to connect two affirmative sentences.

Use **neither do / does** to connect two negative sentences.

Use **but** when one sentence is affirmative and the other is negative.

C GOAL Describe a Special Day

Language Expansion: Special Days

New Year

Independence Day

Diwali

Carnival

Eid

A Look at the photos. Where do you think they are in the world?

B Match the sentences to the photos. Write the numbers on the photos.

1. People celebrate this day in October or November by lighting lamps and candles.

2. In Brazil, people often dress up in costumes for this festival. It's a big party!

3. Chinese people decorate the streets and houses on this special day.

4. In the United States, there are always fireworks at night on this day.

5. Muslims often give presents on this day.

C Complete the sentences with the words in blue from **B**.

1. Diwali is called the ___festival___ of light.

2. We watch the _____ in the sky on New Year's Eve.

3. On Halloween, children dress up in _____.

4. During Diwali, people in India _____ streets and houses in many colors.

5. Mexicans _____ the Day of the Dead from October 31st to November 2nd.

6. I get _____ on my birthday, and I often have a big _____ with my family and friends.

D **MY WORLD** In pairs, discuss the questions about your country.

1. When do you have special days? What do you do?

2. Do you watch fireworks? If so, when?

3. Do you wear costumes? If so, when?

4. Do you give presents? If so, when?

Grammar

E Unscramble the words to make sentences.

1. always / fireworks / we / have / on / New Year's Eve _____

2. Valentine's Day / never / I / send / on / cards _____

3. sometimes / we / neighbors / visit / on / New Year's Day _____

4. I / often / get / on / my / don't / presents / birthday _____

5. usually / it's / Independence Day / hot / on _____

F Take turns. Tell a partner which sentences in **E** are true for you.

Conversation

G 🎧 11 Listen to the conversation about a special day. How do Diego and Chuck show interest? Check (✓) the phrases and questions you hear.

Diego: What do you do on New Year's Eve?

Chuck: Well, we sometimes go downtown. There are always fireworks.

Diego: Really?

Chuck: Yes, it's really pretty. What about you?

Diego: No, we never have fireworks, but we often go to a friend's house.

Chuck: Cool. Do you give presents?

Diego: No, we don't. We do that on Christmas. On New Year's Eve, we just have a big party!

SPEAKING STRATEGY

Showing Interest

☐ Cool!

☐ Do you celebrate / give / go...?

☐ Really?

☐ What do you do on...?

☐ What / How about you?

☐ Where do you go...?

☐ Wow!

H Practice the conversation with a partner. Then switch roles and practice it again.

 GOAL CHECK Describe a Special Day

1. Prepare answers for these questions in your notebook.

- What day is special to you?
- What do you do?
- Who do you spend it with?
- What do you wear?
- Do you have fireworks? Decorations? Presents?

2. In pairs, talk about your special day. Show interest and ask follow-up questions.

D GOAL Talk about Hobbies and Interests

Reading

A What percentage of your day is for...

- sleep? _____%
- work / school? _____%
- free time? _____%

B In pairs, compare your answers in **A**. Do you want more free time for your hobbies and interests? Why?

C Read the article about Leyla and Michael. Which sentence is correct?

  a. Their hobby is also their job.

  b. They like their hobbies, but not their jobs.

  c. They like both their hobbies and their jobs.

D Read the article again and answer the questions.

  1. Why do most people want more free time?

  _____

  2. What does Leyla write about?

  _____

  3. How many people follow her blog?

  _____

  4. What does Michael love doing?

  _____

  5. Who does he run with?

  _____

  6. Where does his company have running tours?

  _____

✓ **GOAL CHECK**

  1. Think about your answers to these questions.

  - What are your hobbies and interests?

  - Why do you like them?

  2. Work in groups and tell each other your answers.

  I love...

  My favorite hobby is...
  I like it because...

  3. **MY WORLD** Do you think your hobby can also be your job someday? How? Tell your group.

Leyla Kazim at a store in Bahrain

When Your Hobby Is Also Your Job

Every day, we eat, sleep, and work, but most people also want more free time for their hobbies and interests. Maybe they want to play more sports, learn a musical instrument, or even write a book, but they don't have the time. It's a problem for many, but the answer is simple when your hobby is also your job!

Leyla Kazim is a good example of how to have a **passion** and make money from it. Leyla loves travel, photography, and food, so she writes a blog. "I spend most of my time either eating, traveling, or creating **content** about the two," she says. Leyla's blog has more than 100,000 followers and, because the blog is so popular, she also works with food companies and restaurants.

Michael Gazaleh is another person with a hobby that's also his job. He loves running in his free time and he also loves showing people his home city of New York. So his company, City Running Tours, gives tours of cities to people who also like running. "Every day, we get to run with wonderful people from all over the world," he says. Michael's company now has running tours in 14 different cities in the US and Canada.

Leyla and Michael both love their job because it's also their hobby. So, do you have a hobby or a passion? How can you make it your job?

passion something you love doing
content information, such as writing, videos, and blog posts, found on a website

GOAL Plan a Party

Communication

A Do you ever have parties at work or at school? Why?

B In small groups, imagine that your English class finishes this week. Plan a small class party. Discuss:

- the day.
- the time.
- the place.
- food and drink.
- a present for your teacher.

C Present your plans for the party to the rest of the class.

> The party is on...

> It's at...

> We want to eat / drink...

> The present is a...

Writing

D Read five emails about a party. Circle **T** for *true* or **F** for *false*.

1. It's Yuka's last day at work today.   **T**   **F**

2. Leticia leaves at five o'clock.   **T**   **F**

3. Yuka buys a card and a present.   **T**   **F**

4. There are flowers for Leticia.   **T**   **F**

5. The party is in a restaurant.   **T**   **F**

Hi Mike,
Do you know Leticia in reception? It's her last day at work today! We need a card and a present for her. Can you buy them?
Best, Yuka

Hi Yuka,
Yes, you're right. Let's celebrate! What time does she finish? I'll buy a card and a cake on my lunch break.
Mike

Hi Mike,
She always leaves at five o'clock. Thanks—I don't have a lunch break today!
Yuka

Hi Yuka,
I have the card and the cake. I also have flowers!
Mike

Hi everyone,
It's Leticia's last day at work today. Let's meet at five o'clock in the reception area for a small party. Mike has a card, flowers, and a cake! See you later.
Yuka

Write these words and phrases from the emails in the table.

Best	Can you help?	Do you know...?	Hi
Let's meet at...	See you later.	Can you buy...?	What time...?

WRITING SKILL: Parts of an Email

Start an email	1. _Hi_____
Ask for help	2. _____
	3. _____
Ask for information	4. _____
	5. _____
Arrange to meet	6. _____
End the email	7. _____
	8. _____

✓ **GOAL CHECK** Plan a Party

Email 1: Someone at work has a birthday today. Write an email to a friend at work.

1. Start the email.
2. Tell him or her about the birthday.
3. Ask for help. (You need a present and a cake.)
4. End the email.

Email 2: Exchange emails with a partner and write a reply.

1. You have the present and the cake.
2. Ask for information about the party. (What time? Where?)

Email 3: Exchange your emails again and write the last email.

1. Arrange to meet.

RUBEN'S ELEVATOR

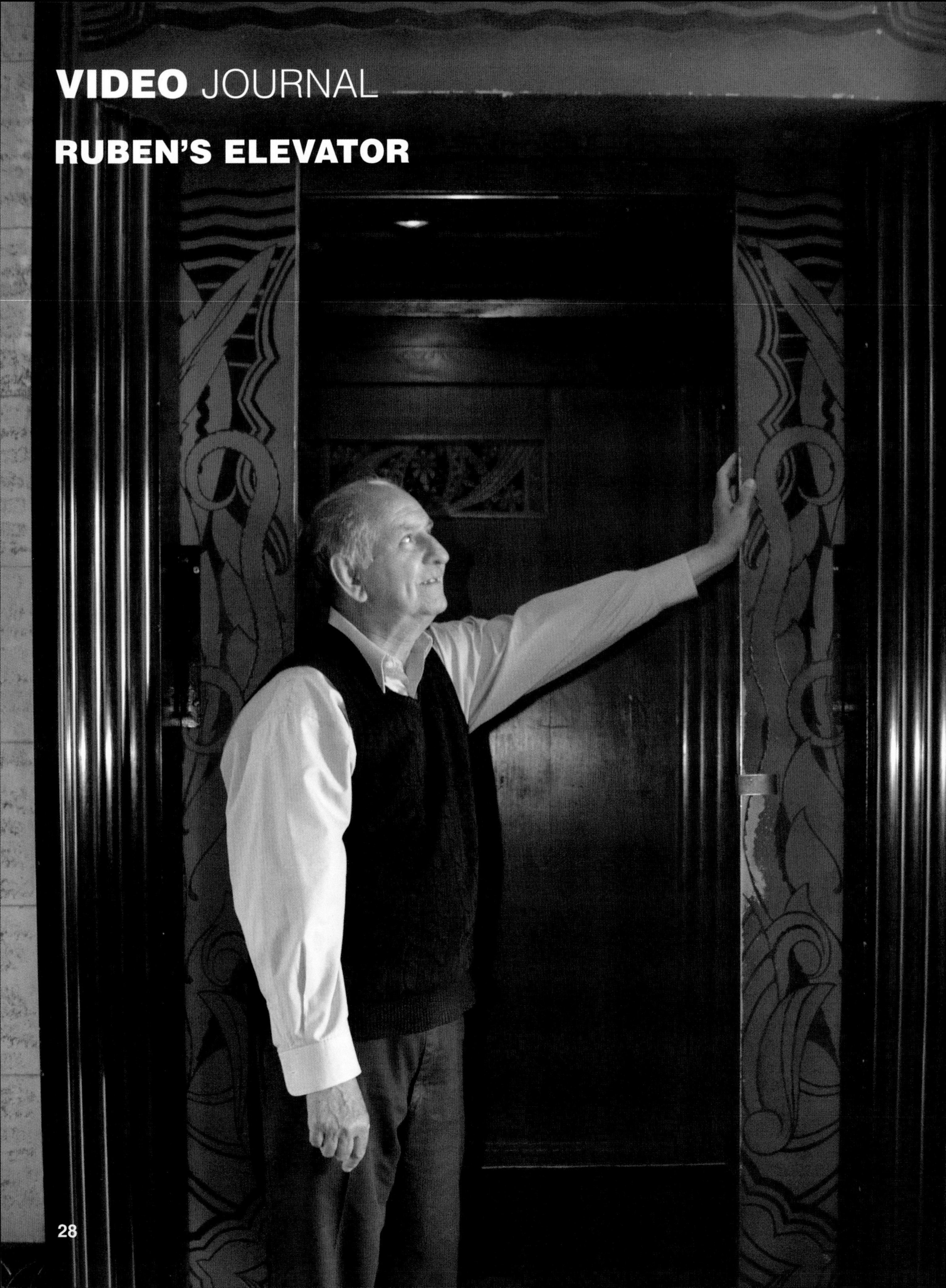

A You are going to watch a video about Ruben Pardo. He is 75 years old, and he's the oldest elevator operator in Los Angeles. Where do you see elevators? What do you think an elevator operator does?

B Do you think it's an interesting job? Why?

C Watch the video. Number the actions from 1 to 8 in the order you see them.

- [1] Ruben opens the doors of a tall building.
- [ ] He sweeps the floor.
- [ ] He says "hello" to a lady.
- [ ] Lots of different people enter the elevator.
- [ ] Ruben asks a man, "How's your day?"
- [ ] He has a cup of coffee.
- [ ] He stops at the second floor.
- [ ] He sits and waits in the elevator.

D Watch the video again. Circle **T** for *true* or **F** for *false*.

1. Ruben knows how to operate elevators from watching old movies.   **T**   **F**

2. His first day at work was August 14, 1966.   **T**   **F**

3. He's worked in the same building for forty years.   **T**   **F**

4. When he stops the elevator, he makes the elevator even with the floor.   **T**   **F**

5. He is the oldest of his brothers and sisters.   **T**   **F**

6. Ruben graduated from college.   **T**   **F**

7. On Sundays, he takes his family out.   **T**   **F**

8. He often feels bored.   **T**   **F**

E Work in small groups. These sentences describe what Ruben does. Which sentences describe a positive point about the job? (Write ✓) Which describe a negative point about the job? (Write X)

1. [ ] He meets lots of different people.
2. [ ] He goes up and down all day.
3. [ ] He cleans the elevator.
4. [ ] Sometimes people give him a tip.
5. [ ] He gets Sundays off.
6. [ ] Usually, it isn't a stressful job.
7. [ ] Sometimes the elevator stops working.
8. [ ] He needs special training.

F Think of a person with a job; for example, you, your teacher, a parent, or a friend. Plan a short video about a normal day at their job from the beginning of the day to the end. Make notes in the table below.

Time of day	What do they do?

G Work in pairs and describe your plan for the video.

Going Places

A taxi driver takes tourists through the streets of Camagüey, Cuba.

Look at the photo and answer the questions.

1 Do you ever take taxis? Why?

2 When you travel, what transportation do you normally use?

UNIT 3 GOALS

A. Talk about Your Possessions

B. Ask for and Give Travel Information

C. Ask for and Give Advice

D. Plan a Vacation

E. Describe a Place

GOAL Talk about Your Possessions

Vocabulary

A Read the to-do list for a vacation. Where is the vacation?

My Vacation
To do
1. Pack:
- Luggage: clothes, sunblock, sunglasses, camera
- Carry-on bag: passport, phone, charger
2. Exchange money: $300 into Thai baht
3. Take taxi to airport
Flight details
Thai Air 768 to Bangkok
Check-in time: 12:05
Flight leaves: 2:05

B Fill in the blanks with words from the to-do list in **A**.

1. _____ your luggage.

2. Don't check in your _____ bag.

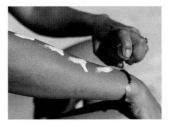

3. Put on _____.

4. Go to the _____ desk.

5. Don't forget your _____ !

6. Take a _____ for your phone.

7. _____ your money.

8. Let's _____ a taxi.

C **MY WORLD** When you travel, what possessions do you take? Tell a partner.

Grammar

Possession				
Possessive *'s*	Possessive Adjective	Possessive Pronoun	*Belong to*	
X	**my**	**mine**		me.
X	**your**	**yours**		you.
Tim**'s** passport	**his**	**his**	It **belongs to**	him.
My sister**'s** bag	**her**	**hers**	They **belong to**	her.
X	**our**	**ours**		us.
My parent**s'** bag	**their**	**theirs**		them.

D Complete the conversations. Use a word or phrase for possession.

1. **A:** Excuse me, is this _____ bag? **B:** No, it's not _____.
2. **A:** Is this Anna's bag? **B:** No, _____ is green.
3. **A:** _____ ticket is this? **B:** I think it _____ Shawn.

REAL LANGUAGE

To ask about possession, we can ask, *Whose... is this?*

E Answer the questions using *belong to* and a possessive pronoun.

1. Whose passport is this? (Ali) _____ *It belongs to Ali. It's his.* _____
2. Whose keys are these? (my) _____
3. Whose camera is this? (my sister) _____
4. Whose bags are these? (John and Lucy) _____
5. Whose tickets are these? (Logan and you) _____

Conversation

F 🎧 13 Listen to the conversation. Who do the items in the box belong to?

> **Anna:** OK, do we have everything? I have my <u>passport</u>. Whose <u>ticket</u> is this?
> **Bill:** It's mine! And those are my <u>sunglasses</u>. Can you pass them to me?
> **Jim:** Sure, here you go. And is this <u>sunblock</u> yours?
> **Bill:** No, it's not mine.
> **Anna:** It's mine. Whose <u>camera</u> is this?
> **Jim:** It's mine. Well, it belongs to <u>my brother</u>, but I need it for our trip.

camera
passport
sunblock
sunglasses
ticket

G Practice the conversation in a group. Switch roles and practice it again. Then change the underlined words and make a new conversation.

 GOAL CHECK Talk about Your Possessions

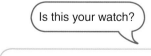

Give a personal item (like your pen or watch) to your teacher. Your teacher will then give you someone else's personal item. Try to find the owner.

GOAL Ask for and Give Travel Information

Listening

A 🎧 14 Listen to the tourist. In which three places do the conversations take place?

☐ Airport check-in ☐ Restaurant ☐ Hotel reception
☐ Immigration ☐ Car rental

WORD FOCUS

tourist a person who
visits a place

B 🎧 14 Listen again and write the missing information.

BOARDING PASS

Destination: _Buenos Aires_   Boarding time: _____

Seat number: _____   Gate number: _____

CAR RENTAL

Booking number: _____

Length of rental: _____ days

Cell phone: _____

Address in Argentina: _____,
Avenida Brasil

HOTEL CHECK-IN

Last name: _____

Number of nights: _____

Single ☐   Double ☐

Room number: _____

**The La Boca neighborhood
of Buenos Aires, Argentina**

PRONUNCIATION: Rising and Falling Intonation

When we ask questions with two options, we use rising and falling intonation. The intonation rises on the first option and falls on the second one.

REAL LANGUAGE

We often check information using questions:

Is it for one night or two? / Is your middle initial A or E?

C 🎧 **15** Listen and repeat. Use rising and falling intonation.

1. Would you like a window ↗ or aisle ↘ seat?   3. Do you spell that L-E-E ↗ or L-I ↘?

2. Is this bag to check in ↗ or carry on ↘?   4. Is it for one night ↗ or two ↘?

D Practice asking these questions with a partner. Use rising and falling intonation.

1. Are you from the US or Canada?
2. Do you want to pay by cash or by card?
3. Is your visit for business or pleasure?
4. Do you want my ticket or my passport?
5. Do you leave on the 25th or the 26th?

Communication

E Ask a partner questions to fill out the information with his or her travel information. For some questions, you might have to make up information.

1. First name _____
2. Middle initial(s) _____
3. Last name _____
4. Date of birth _____
5. Nationality _____
6. Country of residence _____
7. Contact number _____
8. Date of arrival _____
9. Number of nights _____
10. Type of room (single / double?) _____
11. Reason for visit (business / vacation?) _____

 GOAL CHECK
Ask for and Give Travel Information

Work with a new partner. Ask and answer questions about your previous partner using the information in **E**.

What is his last name?   His last name is...   Her contact number is...   She arrives on...

GOAL Ask for and Give Advice

Language Expansion: Describing Places

A Underline the correct adjective in each sentence.

1. There's a *cheap / delicious* hotel near the train station.
2. The weather is hot in the summer and *warm / crowded* in the winter.
3. In the afternoon, lots of people go to the beach, so it's *crowded / quiet*.
4. In Patagonia, the views are *beautiful / warm*.
5. Don't walk around after midnight because it's a *dangerous / cheap* part of town.
6. That restaurant is famous for its *delicious / safe* seafood.
7. England is often very *cold / hot* in the winter.
8. Shopping is very *expensive / ugly* at the airport.

Grammar

Should for Advice							
Should				Questions with *should*			
You	**should** **shouldn't**	take	a camera.	**Should**	I	take	a camera?
Use *should / shouldn't* to give advice.				Use questions with *should* to ask for advice.			

B In pairs, use the words and phrases in the table to give advice for the sentences in **A**.

Example: There's a cheap hotel near the train station. *You should stay there.*

You	should	buy clothes there. eat there. go early in the morning. pack sunblock.
	shouldn't	stay there. take your camera. walk there late at night. wear a warm coat.

C Ask for advice. Read the responses and write questions.

1. **Q:** *Should I take the shuttle bus to the airport?*

   A: Yes, you should. The shuttle bus is quick and cheap.

2. **Q:** _____

   A: No, you shouldn't. It is hot at the beach. You don't need a sweater.

3. **Q:** _____

   A: Yes, you should. It's expensive to exchange it at the airport.

4. **Q:** _____

   A: No, you shouldn't. It's dangerous to carry cash.

D In pairs, take turns asking the questions in **C**. Give different advice.

Conversation

E 🎧 16 Listen to the conversation between two friends about a vacation in Japan. Check (✓) the topics they discuss:

☐ Food ☐ Places to stay ☐ Transportation

☐ Language ☐ Shopping ☐ When to go

F Practice the conversation with a partner. Switch roles and practice it again.

Claudia:	I want to visit Japan next year. Can you give me some advice?
Ayumi:	Sure, it's an interesting country.
Claudia:	Do you think I should go in the summer?
Ayumi:	You can, but it's very hot. I think you should go in the spring. It's a beautiful time of year, and the Japanese gardens are famous.
Claudia:	OK. And do I need to rent a car?
Ayumi:	No, you don't need to. It's a good idea to take trains because they're fast between the big cities.
Claudia:	Right. I fly into Tokyo. Is Tokyo expensive?
Ayumi:	Very! And it's so crowded. Why don't you stay in Fujiyoshida? It's not too far from Tokyo. It's a small city near Mount Fuji and the hotels are nice.

✓ GOAL CHECK Ask for and Give Advice

1. Think about travel advice for your country. Make notes about some of these topics:

Clothing	Hotels	Places to visit	Shopping
Food	Money	Transportation	When to go

2. In pairs, take turns asking for and giving advice.

The view of Mount Fuji from Fujiyoshida, Japan

GOAL Plan a Vacation

Reading

A When you go on vacation, which activities do you like to do? Tell the class.

- ☐ Dance in the evening
- ☐ Eat local food
- ☐ Go camping
- ☐ Go to festivals
- ☐ Go shopping
- ☐ Go sightseeing
- ☐ Meet local people
- ☐ Play sports
- ☐ Suntan on the beach
- ☐ Visit museums

B Read the article. Which activities in **A** are in the article? Check (✓) the boxes.

C Read the article again. Does the author agree or disagree with this advice? Circle **A** for *agree* or **D** for *disagree.*

1. You should plan everything before your vacation. **A   D**

2. Visit new places out of the city center. **A   D**

3. Always buy food from supermarkets. **A   D**

4. Get all your information from guidebooks and the internet. **A   D**

5. Talk to local people for advice and suggestions. **A   D**

D **MY WORLD** Do you agree with the author's advice? Why? Tell a partner.

 GOAL CHECK

In small groups, plan an interesting vacation for friends visiting your country.

1. Your friends have three days in your country. Write down what they can do on each day:

Day one	Day two	Day three

2. Present your plan to another group. Do you think the other group has an interesting vacation?

Make Your Vacation More Interesting

Aziz Abu Sarah *has a travel company and often gives advice to tourists. Here he answers the question: "How can a vacation be more interesting?"*

Don't plan everything

Tourists often study maps and plan everything before they go on vacation. It's fun to go sightseeing, but sometimes it's interesting to leave the map at the hotel. For example, you can leave the city center and visit new places. When I was in Tokyo for the first time, I traveled to the suburbs. Two hours later, I was singing karaoke and dancing with local people.

Try the local food

Eating local food always makes a vacation more interesting. Go to food markets where local people sell fresh food that they grew or cooked. In these places, you learn more about their food and culture. It's much more interesting than going to a supermarket—and the food is better!

Find out where local people go

When you arrive in a new place, find out about festivals and events. Local magazines and posters have information about art galleries and live music. If you like sports, find out where people play. A few years ago, I was in Tunisia and I played soccer on the beach with a group of local men.

Ask for advice and suggestions

All around the world, people are always happy to give advice. Don't always use the guidebook or the internet. Ask local people for suggestions on where to go or where to eat. Once, in Curitiba, Brazil, I asked a local group where I should have dinner in the city. They invited me for dinner and I am still friends with them!

Aziz Abu Sarah at the Matterhorn in Switzerland

E GOAL Describe a Place

Communication

A What is your "dream" vacation? Why?

B You win a vacation for two people and can choose from the three places below. In pairs, discuss the places and choose one. Present and explain your decision to the class.

> Angkor Wat is good…

> I prefer a vacation at the beach.

Angkor Wat, Cambodia	Adventure sports, New Zealand	Bahia beaches, Brazil
The temples at Angkor Wat in Cambodia are from the 12th century and are very beautiful. It's a famous place, so thousands of tourists visit every day.	Tourists come to New Zealand because it has an amazing countryside. It's perfect for canoeing in the rivers and bungee jumping off bridges.	The coast of Bahia is 685 miles long, so you can always find a quiet beach during the day. Then you can go to a beach bar at night and dance until the morning.

C In small groups, read comments from six tourists about vacations. Recommend a vacation from **B** or choose a new vacation. Give reasons.

> This person should choose…

> …because it has…

> …because you can…

1. "I like vacations with exercise and lots of things to do."

2. "After working all year, I want to relax by the ocean."

3. "I like sightseeing and visiting interesting places with a lot of history."

4. "I want to meet new people and go to parties!"

5. "I live in a crowded city, so I want to go to a place with nature and no people."

6. "I always go to the same place. This year, I want to do something exciting!"

Angkor Wat, Cambodia

D **MY WORLD** Think about the six tourists in **C**. Which tourist is most similar to you?

Writing

Action + *because* **+ reason**

Tourists come to New Zealand **because** *it has an amazing countryside.*

Every summer, people go camping in Scotland **because** *it's relaxing and cheap.*

Reason + *so* **+ action**

Angkor Wat is a famous place in Cambodia, **so** *thousands of tourists visit every day.*

The coast of Bahia is 685 miles long, **so** *you can always find a quiet beach.*

E Underline *because* or *so* to complete the sentences.

1. Venice is popular with tourists *because / so* it's a beautiful old city surrounded by water.

2. In Japan, the trains are fast, *because / so* you can travel quickly between cities.

3. New Orleans is crowded in March *because / so* the festival of Mardi Gras is during that month.

4. In some parts of Norway, it is dark for 20 hours a day in the winter, *because / so* visitors should go in the summer.

5. Mexico City has amazing museums, *because / so* it's perfect if you love history.

6. A lot of people visit Peru every year *because / so* it has interesting places and delicious food.

F Look back at the three descriptions in **B**. Check (✓) what they describe.

- ☐ An interesting place for sightseeing
- ☐ A festival or special event
- ☐ The local food and drink
- ☐ Places for relaxation
- ☐ Sports and entertainment

 GOAL CHECK Describe a Place

Write a short description of a different place. Give information about things like sightseeing, festivals, places for relaxation, food, etc. Try to use the conjunctions *because* and *so*.

Cartagena, Colombia, has a lot of beautiful and historic buildings, so it's great for sightseeing. There are a lot of good restaurants, too. People also visit because you can swim or relax in the sun on the beaches nearby.

THE UK IN 100 SECONDS

A Discuss the questions in pairs.

1. What can you see in this photo of the United Kingdom?

2. What are three things you know about the UK?

3. Do you think most of the land in the UK has cities, forests, or farms? Why?

B Watch the video. Circle **T** for *true* or **F** for *false*.

1. The population of the UK is about 66 million. T F

2. People live on about 50% of the land. T F

3. The forest is the man's favorite place. T F

4. Crops use the most land. T F

5. Half of the crops are used for animals. T F

6. At the end of the walk, we see the ocean. T F

The mountain of Blencathra in the Lake District of England.

C Fill in the graph with the information from the video.

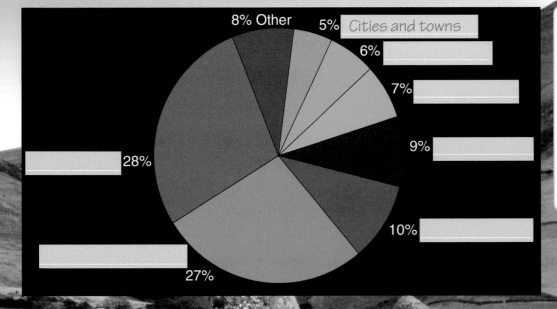

8% Other
5% Cities and towns
6%
7%
9%
28%
10%
27%

Crops and vegetables
Forest
Grasslands
~~Cities and towns~~
Land for farm animals
Moors
Peat bogs

D Watch the video and check your answers in **C**.

E Work in small groups. Answer the questions about your country.

1. What different types of land uses are in your country? E.g. cities, forests etc.

2. What is similar about the land in the UK and your country? What is different?

3. Do you think people should use land in different ways? Why?

F Plan a 100-second video about your country. Make notes about the video below. Then share your ideas with the class.

Time	What do you say?	What do you show?
0–20		
21–40		
41–60		
61–80		
81–100		

WORD FOCUS

crops plants that farmers grow for food

moors open land that cannot be used for farming

peat bog wet land with dead plant material

43

Food

Food is different around the world. This photo shows vegetables, including potatoes, carrots, and radishes.

UNIT 4 GOALS

A. Describe a Recipe

B. Order a Meal

C. Talk about Diets

D. Plan a Farm or Garden

E. Follow and Give Instructions

A GOAL Describe a Recipe

Vocabulary

A In pairs, choose a word or phrase from the box to describe each group of foods.

dairy products   drinks
fruit   meat   vegetables

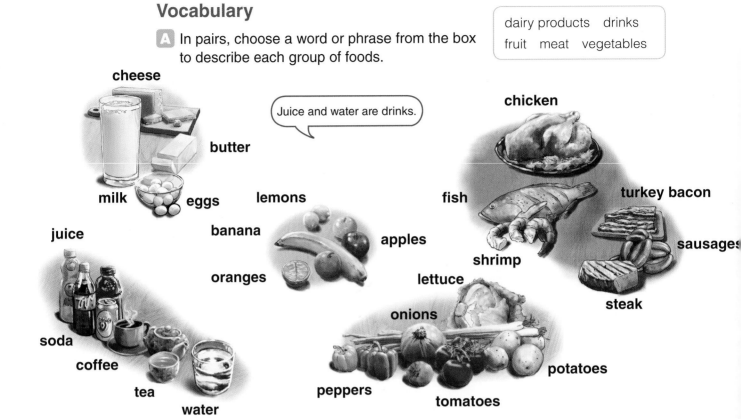

Juice and water are drinks.

cheese
butter
milk   eggs
juice
banana
lemons
oranges
apples
soda
coffee
tea
water
peppers
onions
lettuce
tomatoes
potatoes
chicken
fish
shrimp
turkey bacon
sausages
steak

B In pairs, think of some other foods you know and write them in the correct group. Then share them with the class.

C What are your favorite foods? Choose one from each group.

Grammar

Count and Non-count Nouns	
Singular	Plural
This is **a** lemon. This is milk.	These are lemons. ~~These are milks.~~

a / an, some, and *any*			
	Count Nouns		Non-count Nouns
	Singular	Plural	
Statement	We need **an** apple.	There are **some** apples on the table.	There is **some** cheese on the table.
Negative	I don't have **a** lemon.	There aren't **any** lemons at the store.	We don't have **any** milk.
Question	Do we have **a** red pepper?	Are there **any** red peppers?	Do you have **any** butter?

D In your notebook, make a chart with two columns: *Count nouns* and *Non-count nouns*. Write the food words from **A** and **B** in the correct column.

E 🎧 18 Complete the conversation with *a / an*, *some*, or *any*. Then listen and check.

Lee: I'm hungry. What's in the fridge?

Diana: There are (1) _____ eggs.

Lee: Do you have (2) _____ vegetables?

Diana: Yes, I have (3) _____ onion and (4) _____ red pepper.

Lee: Great! Let's make a Spanish omelet. Do you have (5) _____ olive oil?

Diana: No, but I have (6) _____ corn oil. That should be okay.

Lee: Sure. And we need (7) _____ potatoes.

Diana: I don't have (8) _____ potatoes, but I can go to the store.

Lee: OK, I'll start cooking.

F Practice the conversation in pairs. Switch roles and practice it again.

G In pairs, make two new conversations using the ingredients below. Use the conversation in **E** as a model.

Quiche	Frittata
• eggs	• butter
• cheese	• eggs
• milk	• cheese
• onion	• turkey bacon
• salt and pepper	• tomato

H Think of a popular dish in your country and write down the ingredients.

 GOAL CHECK Describe a Recipe

Tell a partner the name of your dish and ask them for the ingredients you need to make it.

Let's make...

I need some...

Do you have any...?

I don't have any...

I have a...

B GOAL Order a Meal

Listening

A 🎧 19 Listen to a conversation in a restaurant. Write the man's and woman's order in the chart below.

	Drink	Food
Man		
Woman		

B 🎧 19 Who asked these questions, the man, the woman, or the waiter? Write your answers. Then listen again to check.

1. Can we order our drinks first? _____man_____

2. Do you have any mineral water? _____

3. Would you like sparkling or still? _____

4. Are you ready to order? _____

5. Would you like an appetizer? _____

6. Does the steak come with a salad? _____

7. How would you like your steak? _____

8. Would you like anything else? _____

C 🎧 20 Read the information. Then listen to the full and reduced forms of the questions.

PRONUNCIATION: Reduced forms: *Do you have...* and *Would you like...*

In natural speech, *Do you have...* and *Would you like...* are often reduced at the beginning of questions. This means that some sounds change, or are not said at all.

1. Do you have any oranges?	2. Would you like some milk?
Full: /du ju hæv/	Full: /wʊd ju laɪk/
Reduced: /dəjə hæv/	Reduced: /wʊdʒə laɪk/

D 🎧 21 Listen and check (✓) the correct column. Then listen again and repeat.

	Full Form	Reduced Form
1. Do you have any mineral water?		
2. Would you like sparkling or still?		
3. Would you like anything else?		
4. Do you have any iced tea?		
5. Would you like some coffee?		

Communication

People eat at an outdoor cafe in Michoacán, Mexico.

E Complete the menu with the words in the box.

MENU

(1) __Appetizers__

Garlic bread, cheese plate,

vegetable (2) _____

---

(3) _____

New York steak and salad,

chicken and French fries,

Italian (4) _____

---

(5) _____

Strawberries and ice cream,

chocolate cake, lemon pie

---

(6) _____

Mineral water, iced tea,

(7) _____

---

appetizers
coffee
desserts
drinks
main dishes
pizza
soup

F In pairs, write the name of another dish or drink at the bottom of each section of the menu.

 GOAL CHECK Order a Meal

1. In pairs, use the menu and role-play a conversation between a waiter and a customer.

   Student A: You are the waiter. Take the customer's order. Then read the order back to them.

   Student B: You are the customer. Order a meal from the menu.

2. Change roles and repeat the role play.

Would you like...?

Do you have...?

I'd like...

So that's...

GOAL Talk about Diets

Language Expansion: Diets

A Compare the two meals and say which is healthier. Why?

B Match these pairs of words to the correct comment.

1. Fast food / Healthy

   a. "People say burgers and fries are bad for you, but I only eat them once a week." __Fast food__

   b. "My doctor says I should eat more fruit and vegetables." __Healthy__

2. Home grown / Processed

   a. "I'd love to cook, but I don't have time. After work, I often buy ready-made meals that you put in the microwave." _____

   b. "Gardening is hard work, but your own fruit tastes much better than fruit from the supermarket." _____

3. Vegetarian / Vegan

   a. "I don't eat meat. I eat a lot of dairy products, fruit, and vegetables instead." _____

   b. "I don't eat anything from animals, like meat, milk, or cheese." _____

4. High-fiber / High-protein

   a. "My diet has lots of meat and fish. I don't eat bread or rice." _____

   b. "I'm on a special diet with lots of wheat bread and brown rice." _____

5. Packaged / Fresh

   a. "The apples are from the farm. They're delicious!" _____

   b. "The label says it has a lot of extra salt in it." _____

6. Organic / Frozen

   a. "I want to eat food with no man-made additives, but it's more expensive." _____

   b. "There's some ice cream in the freezer for dessert." _____

C In pairs, say one more type of food for each category.

   Fast food: fried chicken
   Healthy food: nuts

Grammar

How much and How many with Quantifiers

Information Questions		Quantifiers		
		++++	+	−
Count	**How many** oranges do you need?	I need **lots / a lot of** oranges.	I need **a few** oranges.	I don't need **many** oranges.
Non-count	**How much** bread do we have?	We have **lots / a lot of** bread.	We have **a little** bread.	We don't have **much** bread.

Questions	Short Answers
How many do you need?	**A lot. / A few. / Not many.**
How much do we have?	**A lot. / A little. / Not much.**

D Underline the correct word.

1. **A:** How *much / many* potatoes would you like? **B:** Just *a little / a few*, thanks.
2. **A:** How *much / many* steak do we need? **B:** There are nine of us, so we need *lots of / a little* steak.
3. **A:** How *much / many* rice can you eat? **B:** Not *much / many*. I'm on a high-protein diet.
4. **A:** How *much / many* sugar do you want? **B:** I only take *a little / a few* in my coffee.
5. **A:** How *much / many* eggs are in the fridge? **B:** There aren't *much / many*. Just one or two, I think.

E 🎧 22 Write the missing words in this conversation. Listen to check your answers. What words describe Pat's new diet?

Kim: Hi Pat. You look great!
Pat: Thanks! It's my new diet.
Kim: Really? What do you eat?
Pat: (1) _____ of meat and fish, but I don't eat (2) _____ bread. Oh, and I eat a (3) _____ vegetables, of course.
Kim: (4) _____ much fruit can you eat?
Pat: Just a (5) _____ after every meal.
Kim: What about snacks?
Pat: Well, I can eat a (6) _____ nuts, and sometimes I eat a (7) _____ chocolate, but it's organic, so there isn't (8) _____ added sugar in it.
Kim: Mmm, sounds good! Maybe I'll try your diet.

F Practice the conversation in pairs. Switch roles and practice again.

G Think about your own diet or a special diet you know about. Make a list of:
- food you normally eat (or you can eat).
- food you don't eat (or you can't eat).

*What **do** you eat every day?* = What's your typical diet?
*What **can** you eat on this diet?* = What are you allowed to eat on this special diet?

Talking about Quantities
How much / many (meat / vegetables) do / can you eat?
 Just a little / few.
 I don't / can't eat much / many...

Do / Can you eat lots of...?
 Yes, lots of... / Yes, a lot.
 No, not much / many.

✓ **GOAL CHECK** Talk about Diets

In pairs, ask and answer questions about your diet, or a special diet you know. Use your list from **G**.

D GOAL Plan a Farm or Garden

Reading

A In pairs, say three things you can see in the photo.

B Read the article and answer the questions.

1. Who is the photographer?

2. What do his photos show?

3. Where can you eat fresh vegetables and watch baseball?

4. Who takes once a week classes in gardening?

5. How many people live in the world's cities?

C Match the words from the article to the definitions.

1. urban _____
2. farm _____
3. garden _____
4. to grow _____
5. to plant _____
6. volunteers _____
7. therapeutic _e_
8. healthy _____

a. a large area of land for growing food

b. to put something in the ground to grow

c. an area of land with flowers, fruit, and vegetables

d. good for your body

e. good for mental health

f. in the city

g. to increase in size

h. people who work for free

D MY WORLD Ask and answer the questions in small groups.

1. Do you have a garden or farm? If yes, what do you grow?

2. Are you a volunteer? What do you do?

3. What healthy activities do you do in your free time? Are they also therapeutic?

✓ GOAL CHECK

In a small group, plan an urban farm or garden.

1. Say why your city needs an urban farm or garden.

2. Discuss its location.

3. List the types of plants you will grow.

4. Make a poster to advertise your urban farm or garden. Show the location and list your food.

5. Present your poster to the class.

Urban Farming

Volunteers work at the White House garden.

Mario Wezel is a German photographer who takes photos for National Geographic. Mario is interested in urban farming, so many of his photos show farmers and gardeners. However, urban farming is different from traditional farming. It's when people farm and garden in the middle of the city.

Mario traveled to urban farms all over the US. In Boston, one man has bees on the roof of the Lenox Hotel. The hotel uses honey from the bees in its restaurant. In San Francisco, there's a small farm next to the Giants' baseball stadium. When people watch the game, they can also buy sandwiches from the farm with fresh vegetables! And in Washington, DC, volunteers can help in a garden at the White House.

For Mario, the most surprising urban farm is at San Quentin State Prison, in California. The prison has a garden and, once a week, prisoners can take a gardening class. They learn how to grow plants and flowers. Working in the garden is also therapeutic.

Mario's photos are all of the US, but you can find urban farms in a lot of different countries and large cities, such as Tokyo, Lima, and Perth. That's because about 3.5 billion people (half the world's population) live in cities today and they want fresh, healthy food. And more and more people think urban farming is the answer to the world's food **shortages**, as well as to making our cities greener and more relaxing.

shortages when there is not enough of something

GOAL Follow and Give Instructions

Communication

A Read the instructions for *The Food Game*. Then play the game in small groups.

First, go to the START square. Next, take turns flipping a coin. Move 1 square for heads or 2 squares for tails. Then, follow the instructions on the square. Finally, the first person to reach FINISH is the winner.

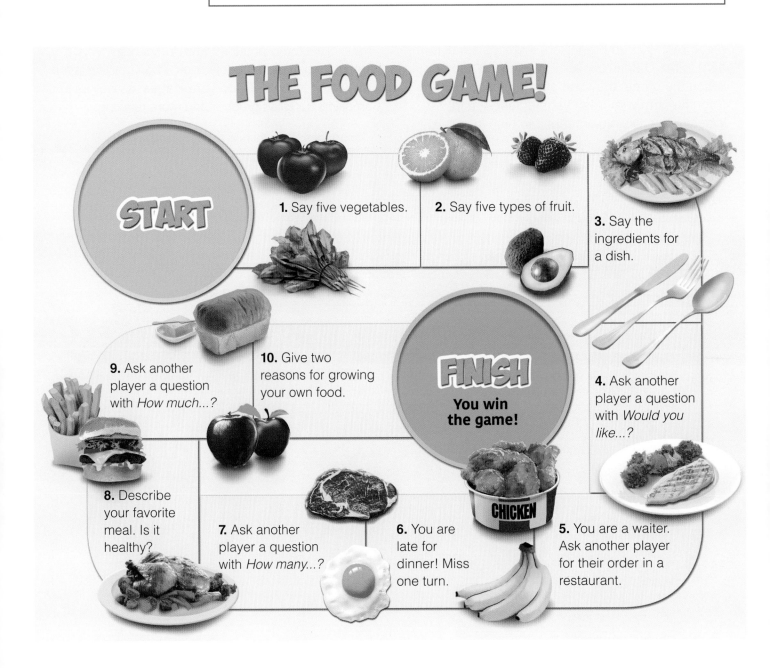

THE FOOD GAME!

START

1. Say five vegetables.

2. Say five types of fruit.

3. Say the ingredients for a dish.

4. Ask another player a question with *Would you like...?*

5. You are a waiter. Ask another player for their order in a restaurant.

6. You are late for dinner! Miss one turn.

7. Ask another player a question with *How many...?*

8. Describe your favorite meal. Is it healthy?

9. Ask another player a question with *How much...?*

10. Give two reasons for growing your own food.

FINISH
You win the game!

Writing

Use sequencing words to give instructions:
First,...
Next,...
Then,...
After (that),...
Meanwhile,... (= at the same time)
Finally, / Last of all,...

Note: We normally use a comma after a sequencing word: *First, you need to. . .*

B Read the instructions for the game again. Underline the sequencing words.

C Put these instructions in the correct order for a recipe for *spaghetti Bolognese*.

_____ After that, take the pasta out of the water.

_____ Finally, it's ready to eat!

_____ Meanwhile, heat the Bolognese sauce in a pan.

_____ First, heat some water in a pot.

_____ Then, put the pasta and the sauce on the plates.

_____ Next, put the pasta in the pot for ten minutes.

D Complete the sequencing words in these instructions.

Hi! Would you like to have dinner at my house? It's easy to get here.
(1) F_____, take the train to the main station. (2) T_____, take bus number 36 to the movie theater. (It takes about 5 minutes.) (3) A_____ t_____, walk down Decatur Avenue. (4) F_____, turn left on Port Street. My house is number 15.

 GOAL CHECK Follow and Give Instructions

1. Choose one of these:
   - Instructions for a recipe
   - Instructions for a game
   - Instructions to get to your house

2. Write your instructions using sequencing words.

3. Exchange instructions with a partner. Can you understand each other's instructions?

TEDTALKS

A GUERRILLA GARDENER IN SOUTH CENTRAL LA

A Read the title and look at the photo of gardener, activist, and TED Talk speaker, Ron Finley. Read the caption. Then answer the questions.

1. Where does he have gardens? (on a farm? in the city?)

2. Why do you think his gardens are important?

3. Do you think people help him? Why?

RON FINLEY
Activist, Gardener

Ron Finley's **IDEA WORTH SPREADING** is that we need to get smarter about the food we eat; and we should start by growing our own. Watch Finley's full TED Talk on TED.com

B Watch the TED Talk. Check (✓) the items you see in the talk.

___ children and teenagers

✓ an empty fridge

___ fast food restaurants

___ George Washington Carver

___ money

___ a parking lot

___ potatoes

___ a shovel

___ a soccer game

___ two beans

___ vacant lots

___ volunteers

C Ron talks about the following things. Number them in the order (1–7) he talks about them. Then, watch again to check.

_1_ He plants his first garden outside his house.

___ He meets a hungry mother and daughter in his garden at night.

___ He starts his volunteer group, LA Green Grounds.

___ Green Grounds now has around 20 gardens.

___ His gardens educate children.

___ He tells people "Grow your own food!"

___ He starts a garden in a homeless shelter.

D In pairs, explain how Ron's gardens solve each problem.

1. Some people in South Central LA are unhealthy because of a poor diet.

2. There are few supermarkets in South Central LA.

3. The city has a lot of vacant lots.

4. Kids do not have a sustainable way of living.

E Write down one problem in your town or city. In small groups, take turns describing the problem and suggesting solutions.

Some people don't have…

People cannot…

My town doesn't have…

Why don't we…?

Ron Finley in his garden

57

A group of children are playing
soccer in Chefchaouen, Morocco.

Look at the photo and answer the questions.

1 What is this sport? Do you like it?

2 What sports do you play? Where do you play them?

UNIT 5 GOALS

A. Describe Activities Happening Now

B. Compare Everyday and Present-Time Activities

C. Talk about Your Favorite Sports

D. Compare Sports and Activities

E. Write and Complete a Questionnaire

GOAL Describe Activities Happening Now

Vocabulary

A Read the text messages. Use the words in blue to label the photos.

> Hi! What are you doing?

> We're at the beach. Kenny's swimming and the others are playing soccer. I'm jogging by the ocean. It's a beautiful day! Are you coming?

> Sorry, I'm not. I'm at Eagle Rocks with Antonia and Pete. They're climbing and I'm hiking. I'm sending you a photo now.

> Wow! The view is amazing! Do people often go skiing there?

> Yes, they do. And I usually go snowboarding here in the winter.

> That sounds amazing!

1. _____

2. _____

3. _____

4. _____

5. _____

6. _____

7. _____

B Write the sports in **A** next to the clues. Some clues have more than one answer.

1. You do these sports on a mountain: _____

2. You can do this sport in a pool: _____

3. You play this sport with a ball: _____

4. This sport is like running: _____

5. You do these sports in the winter: _____

C Think of a sport. Write some clues about it. Then read your clues to a partner. Can they guess your sport?

Grammar

Present Continuous		
Statement	I**'m jogging**	(now).
Negative	He **isn't jogging**	
Yes / No Questions	**Are** they **climbing**	(now)?
Wh- Questions	What **are** you **doing**	
Form the present continuous with *be* + verb + *-ing*. Use the present continuous to talk about things that are happening now (or around the time of speaking).		

D Complete the messages with the present continuous.

Hana: Hi! What (1) _are you doing_ (you / do)?

Pedro: I'm with Ben. We (2) _____ (play) tennis. Are you at the gym?

Hana: No, I (3) _____ (not / go) to the gym today.

Pedro: Why not?

Hana: I have a test tomorrow, so I (4) _____ (study) at home.

Pedro: OK. Good luck!

E Practice the conversation in **D** in pairs.

F Make a new conversation using other sports and activities.

G Work in groups. One student acts out a sport or activity. The other students guess the answer. Use the present continuous.

 GOAL CHECK Describe Activities Happening Now

Answer the questions in pairs.

1. What are you and your partner doing now?

2. What is your teacher doing now?

3. What is your family doing now?

GOAL Compare Everyday and Present-Time Activities

Listening

A In pairs, say what the people in each photo are doing.

B 🎧 24 Listen to three phone calls. Match each call to two photos. Write the number on the photo.

C 🎧 24 Listen again. In pairs, fill in the information below. Each of you fill in one section. Then tell your partner your answers.

Student A: What do these people usually do? When?

1. Alan and Karen usually _____ on _____.

2. Khaled usually _____ in _____.

3. Liam usually _____ on _____.

Student B: What are these people doing now?

1. Alan and Karen _____.

2. Khaled _____.

3. Liam _____.

D Compare these sentences from the phone calls and answer the questions.

    a. I'm ice skating with Alan.   **b.** You usually go to the movies on Fridays.

1. Which sentence uses the simple present? _____

2. Which sentence uses the present continuous? _____

3. Which sentence is about an action happening now (or around the time of speaking)? _____

4. Which sentence is about a habit or routine? _____

E Underline the correct verb form in these sentences.

1. I *play* / *'m playing* tennis now. Can I call you back?

2. We usually *swim* / *are swimming* on Tuesdays and Fridays.

3. They *don't meet* / *aren't meeting* us. They're too busy today.

4. My sister *doesn't get* / *isn't getting* much exercise at the moment. She has her final exams.

F 🎧 25 Read the information. Then listen to the full and reduced forms of the question *What are you doing?*

> **PRONUNCIATION**: Reduced Form of *What are you...*
>
> In natural speech, the question *What are you...?* is often reduced. It sounds like *Whatcha...?*
> Full: /wʌt ɑr ju/ Reduced: /wʌtʃə/

G 🎧 26 Listen and check (✓) the form you hear. Then, listen again and repeat.

	Full Form	Reduced Form
1. What are you doing?		
2. What are you studying?		
3. What are you playing?		
4. What are you writing?		

Communication

 Match the questions to the answers.

1. What are you doing? _____
2. What do you do? _____
3. Where do you go for exercise? _____
4. Do you go skiing in the winter? _____
5. Are you studying a lot at the moment? _____
6. Do you often eat out? _____

a. I'm a doctor.
b. Yes, I am. I have final exams in two weeks!
c. No, not often. It's expensive and I like cooking.
d. I'm studying math.
e. Sometimes, but I usually go snowboarding.
f. To a local gym. And I go running in the park.

I In pairs, take turns asking the questions in **H** and giving your own answers.

✓ **GOAL CHECK** Compare Everyday and Present-Time Activities

1. Write three questions about everyday activities using the simple present, and three questions about present-time activities using the present continuous.

2. In pairs, ask and answer your questions.

What are you reading...

Where do you usually...?

Are you...?

Do you...?

GOAL Talk about Your Favorite Sports

Language Expansion: Team and Individual Sports

A Write the following sports in the correct box, according to the categories.

baseball   football   golf   gymnastics   ice hockey   skateboarding   volleyball   yoga

	Indoor	Outdoor
Team	**basketball** 1. _____ 2. _____	**soccer** 1. _____ 2. _____
Individual	**swimming** 1. _____ 2. _____	**skiing** 1. _____ 2. _____

We use **play** for competitive sports with a ball: *play soccer*
We use **go** for sports with *-ing*: *go swimming*
We use **do** for individual sports with no ball or for relaxation: *do yoga*

B Write the names of more sports in the table.

play	*soccer,*
go	*swimming,*
do	*yoga,*

Grammar

Stative Verbs			
like	Why do you **like** outdoor sports?	know	You **know** I can't swim.
hate	I **hate** indoor sports.	want	I don't **want** to go bungee jumping.
think	I **think** indoor sports are boring.	need	You **need** a lot of equipment.
prefer	Do you **prefer** outdoor sports?	cost	The equipment **costs** a lot of money.

*We usually do not use stative verbs in the present continuous:
~~I am hating outdoor sports.~~ I hate outdoor sports.

C Complete the sentences with the stative verbs in the box.

1. I _____ to play sports more than watch them.

2. My clothes _____ a lot of money.

3. I think rock climbing _____ exciting.

4. My friends and I _____ watching golf on TV. It's so slow!

5. One day I _____ to be a famous athlete.

cost
hate
like
looks
want

WORD FOCUS

An **athlete** is good at sports and physical activities.

D Which sentences in **C** are true for you? Rewrite the untrue sentences so they are true for you. In pairs, read your sentences.

Conversation

E 🎧 27 Listen to the conversation. Does Adrian want to try rock climbing?

Adrian: Why do you like rock climbing?

Kris: I hate being inside all the time. I prefer outdoor sports.

Adrian: Me, too, but it looks dangerous. I don't want to fall.

Kris: Me, neither! That's why we use ropes.

Adrian: Do you need a lot of equipment?

Kris: Yes, you do, and it costs a lot of money.

Adrian: So it's expensive *and* dangerous! I don't think it's for me!

F Practice the conversation in pairs. Switch roles and practice again. Then change the sport and make a new conversation.

SPEAKING STRATEGY

Talking about Likes and Dislikes
Do you like...?
Why do you like...?
Do you prefer... or...?
I like / prefer...
My favorite is...
I hate / don't like...
I'm not interested in...
Me, too!
Me, neither.

✓ GOAL CHECK Talk about Your Favorite Sports

1. Think of your favorite sport. Write answers to these questions.

   - What is the sport?
   - Where do you do it?
   - Do you need special equipment?
   - Does it cost a lot of money?
   - Why do you like it?

2. In pairs, talk about your favorite sports using your answers to the questions. Say if you like your partner's sport.

D **GOAL** Compare Sports and Activities

Reading

A Look at the photo. What are the people watching?

B Read the article. Are the statements *true* or *false*?

1. Online gamers can play against people they don't know.

2. Professional eSports is usually an individual sport.

3. eSports make a lot of money.

4. eSports players get a lot of exercise.

C Are eSports popular in your country? Do you think they are a real sport? Tell the class.

D Match these words from the text to a definition.

1. compete _____
   a. a large place where people watch sports

2. fan _____
   b. type of business

3. industry _____
   c. person who likes a sport

4. sponsor _____
   d. play a sport or game against another person or team

5. stadium _____
   e. give money to sports teams to advertise your product

E **MY WORLD** In pairs, discuss the questions.

1. What is your country's most famous sports team? Are you a fan of the team?

2. Where does the team normally play?

F Read the sentences. Decide if they describe:

a. eSports   **b.** normal sports   **c.** both

1. Played in a large stadium _____

2. The winners receive a prize. _____

3. Players are physically active. _____

4. Players sit in chairs. _____

5. Players need a lot of skill. _____

 GOAL CHECK

In groups, choose two of these sports and activities. Say how they are similar and how they are different.

chess	eSports	rock climbing
skiing	soccer	tennis

Fans cheer at an eSports tournament in Paris, France.

eSports Go Global

In the past, people played computer games in their living rooms and bedrooms against their family and friends. But nowadays, gamers play online against hundreds of different people around the world. There are also millions of fans who love watching these eSports as well as playing. They pay money to watch the very best gamers compete in large stadiums. It's just like watching a real sport!

Like other sports

"eSports" is short for *electronic sports* and, as with normal sports such as soccer and tennis, **professional** eSports players are very competitive. Like real athletes, the best eSports players can train for up to 14 hours a day. In some countries, like China and South Korea, there are competitions in stadiums with up to 80,000 fans. At these events, some of the eSports are individual, but most of them are team games. There are five players on each team and the winning team shares the **prize** money.

Big business

As eSports are growing in popularity, they are also becoming profitable. Globally, the eSports industry is worth about a billion dollars. Large companies sponsor the competitions, and some soccer teams also have their own eSports teams.

But is it a sport?

Of course, some people don't believe it's a real sport because eSports players sit in chairs and they are not physically active. But eSports fans disagree. The players need a lot of skill to win the competitions and, in the future, some people even think eSports will be part of the Olympic Games.

professional a person is *professional* if they earn money doing something
prize what you receive when you win (e.g., money, a trophy)

GOAL Write and Complete a Questionnaire

Communication

A Do you ever go to a gym or health club? Why?

B Read the questionnaire. Answer the two questions.

1. Why do they want information from their customers?

2. What type of information do they want?

We want to offer you the best services at our health club. Please spend 5 minutes answering the questions. Thank you for your time.

1. Which services do you use?

   ☐ The gym ☐ Fitness classes ☐ Swimming pool

   ☐ Basketball court ☐ Sauna and massage

2. How often do you use the gym and health club?

   ☐ More than three times a week ☐ Three times a week

   ☐ Twice a week ☐ Once a week ☐ Less than once a week

3. When do you usually visit the gym and health club?

   ☐ In the morning ☐ Around noon ☐ In the afternoon

   ☐ In the evening

4. Why do you visit the gym and health club?

   ☐ To stay in shape ☐ To lose weight ☐ To have fun and meet people

   ☐ Other? _____

5. How happy are you with the following?

The equipment	☐ Very happy	☐ Happy	☐ Not happy
The fitness classes	☐ Very happy	☐ Happy	☐ Not happy
The staff	☐ Very happy	☐ Happy	☐ Not happy
The price	☐ Very happy	☐ Happy	☐ Not happy
The cafe	☐ Very happy	☐ Happy	☐ Not happy

6. Would you recommend our gym and health club to a friend? Yes / No

   Please give reasons for your answer: _____

   _____

C Work in pairs.

Student A: You work for the gym. Ask Student B the questions and complete the questionnaire.

Student B: You are a customer at the gym. Answer the questions.

Exercise equipment in a gym. Would you like to use this gym? Why?

Writing

WRITING SKILL: Types of Questions

Closed (*Yes / No*) questions	Open (*Wh- / How*) questions
Do you (use / like / visit)...?	What do you...?
Is / Are there...?	Which services do you...?
Would you (recommend / use / play)...?	When / Where / Why do you...?
Can you...?	How often do you...?
	How happy are you with...?

 D Look at the questions in the health club questionnaire and categorize them as closed or open. Which type of question is used the most? Why?

E Complete the questions for a questionnaire about a cafe.

1. _____ do you normally order at our cafe?

2. _____ do you normally visit?

3. _____ do you choose our cafe?

4. _____ do you come here?

5. _____ are you with our customer service?

6. _____ you _____ our cafe to your friends?

✓ **GOAL CHECK** Write and Complete a Questionnaire

1. In groups, choose which group you will write a questionnaire for.

   • visitors to a restaurant   • employees at a company

   • students at a school   • travelers with an airline

2. Write a questionnaire with 6–7 questions. Then exchange your questionnaire with another group and answer the questions.

VIDEO JOURNAL

FREE SOLOING WITH ALEX HONNOLD

A What is Alex Honnold doing in the photo?

B Answer the questions with the adjectives in the box and your own words.

dangerous	difficult	easy	enjoyable
exciting	frightening	fun	individual
interesting	physical	safe	

1. How do you think Alex describes his sport?

2. How would you describe this sport?

C Watch the video about Alex. Number these actions in the order you see them.

- [ ] Alex is driving to Yosemite Park.
- [ ] He's eating breakfast.
- [ ] He's at the top.
- [ ] He's putting on his shoes.
- [ ] He's standing in front of his camper.
- [ ] He's standing on the ledge of Half Dome.

D Underline the correct answer. Then watch again and check your answers.

1. Free soloing is climbing *with* / *without* ropes.

2. Alex likes free soloing because *it's safer* / *you can move more quickly*.

3. With free soloing, you die if you make one *wrong move* / *correct move*.

4. One side of Half Dome in Yosemite Park is like *a wall* / *stairs*.

5. At one moment, Alex asks, *"Why am I doing this?"* / *"What am I doing?"*

6. Alex spends many months *working with other people* / *planning and training*.

E Work in pairs. Watch the video without sound. Describe what Alex is doing. How many present continuous sentences can you make? You can use some of the verbs below.

climb	do	drive	eat
move	put on	stand	

F Imagine you are a journalist. Write five questions for Alex Honnold.

G Work in pairs to complete the interview. Then switch roles and repeat the exercise.

Student A: You are a journalist. Ask your five questions.

Student B: You are Alex Honnold. Answer the questions.

Alex Honnold on Half Dome
in Yosemite National Park,
California, US

Destinations

The ancient city of
Bagan in Myanmar has
over 2,000 buildings.

Look at the photo and answer the questions.

1 Where is Bagan? Would you like to visit a place like this?

2 What are popular destinations for tourists in your country?

UNIT 6 GOALS

A. Describe Past Vacations

B. Ask about a Trip

C. Talk about Your Weekend

D. Describe an Ancient Place

E. Find and Share Information Online

GOAL Describe Past Vacations

Vocabulary

A Match each verb to a noun. Then match each verb + noun to a photo.

buy	change	eat	a car	a famous place	a hotel
go on	pack	rent	local food	money	~~a photo~~
see	stay at	~~take~~	souvenirs	a suitcase	a tour

1. _take a photo_

2. _____

3. _____

4. _____

5. _____

6. _____

7. _____

8. _____

9. _____

B Write the activities you do *before* and *during* your vacation in the correct column.

Before	During

C In groups, write other things you do before and during a vacation. Then share your ideas with the class.

Grammar

Simple Past

	Regular Verbs	Irregular Verbs
Statements	I stay**ed** at a hotel. / We rent**ed** a car.	I **went** on a tour. (go) / We **bought** souvenirs. (buy)
Negative	I **didn't stay** at a hotel.	I **didn't go** on a tour.
Yes / No Questions	**A: Did** you **go** to Asia last year? **B:** Yes, I **did**. / No, I **didn't**.	
Information Questions	**A:** Where **did** you **go** for your vacation last year? **B:** I **went** to Asia.	

D 🎧 30 Complete the text using the simple past of the verbs in the box. Then listen and check your answers.

> buy   fly   go   rent   see   spend   take   visit

Last year, we (1) _____went_____ to Mexico for our vacation. We

(2) _____ to Mexico City from Chicago and stayed

at a hotel in the center. One day, we (3) _____ the

subway to Chapultepec Park and visited the zoo. In the middle of

the week, we flew to Cancun and (4) _____ a

lot of time on the beach. We also took a tour to Merida and

(5) _____ the old city. It was beautiful and I

(6) _____ a lot of souvenirs! Finally, we

(7) _____ a car and (8) _____ Uxmal.

The pyramids were amazing!

The Pyramid of the Magician in Uxmal, Yucatán, Mexico

E In pairs, make sentences about a past vacation. Change the verbs into the simple past.

1. Last summer, / my family / go on / vacation. *Last summer, my family went on vacation.*

2. We / drive / all day.

3. In the evening, / we / arrive / at the campsite

4. Every day, / I / swim / in a lake / and / walk / in the forest.

5. One day, / we / take / a tour of an old city.

✓ GOAL CHECK Describe Past Vacations

1. Think about your favorite vacation. Write sentences about what you did. Describe some of the following:

   - the place or country
   - the accommodations (hotel, campsite)
   - tours and sightseeing
   - activities (e.g., relaxing, swimming)
   - transportation
   - the food
   - shopping

2. In pairs, describe your favorite vacation using your sentences.

GOAL Ask about a Trip

Listening

A Look at the different types of vacations. Which can you see in the photo? Which types of vacations do you like? Why?

> adventure and safari   beach   camping   cruise
>
> sightseeing and guided tour   skiing   theme park

B 🎧 31 Listen to two conversations about two different types of vacations. Write the types of vacations.

Conversation 1: _____   Conversation 2: _____

C 🎧 31 Listen again. Circle **T** for *true* or **F** for *false*. Correct the false statements in your notebook.

Conversation 1			Conversation 2		
1. Mike had a long vacation.	T	F	6. Ellie took a day trip to Orlando.	T	F
2. Chen went to Tanzania.	T	F	7. Ellie visited five theme parks.	T	F
3. He took a boat to an island.	T	F	8. She didn't like Sea World.	T	F
4. Chen climbed up Mount Kilimanjaro.	T	F	9. She went on the Spider-Man ride.	T	F
5. He photographed animals.	T	F	10. Mike wants to go there.	T	F

PRONUNCIATION: Sounds of *-ed* endings

Regular simple past verbs have three endings.
/d/ when the verb ends in a voiced sound (*-p, -f, -k, -s, -x, -sh, -ch, -th*).
/t/ when the verb ends in a voiceless sound (*-b, -v, -g, -z, -j, -th, -l, -m, -n, -r, -w,* and all vowels).
/ɪd/ when the verb ends in /t/ or /d/.

A herd of elephants in Tanzania

D 🎧 32 Listen and check (✓) the correct boxes in the chart. Then listen again and repeat the words.

	/d/	/t/	/ɪd/
packed		✓	
traveled	✓		
wanted			✓
arrived			
liked			
visited			

E 🎧 33 Listen to the sentences and check (✓) the pronunciation of the -ed endings.

	/d/	/t/	/ɪd/
We **stayed** in a hotel			
I **packed** my bags.			
We **rented** a car.			

F Look at exercise **D** on page 75. Read the text aloud and practice saying the simple past verb endings correctly.

Communication

G Make questions from the two conversations in **C** with these words.

1. go / where / did / you _____

2. did / fly to / which airport / you _____

3. did you / there / stay / how long _____

4. see / did / what / you _____

5. did / take / any photos / you _____

6. theme parks / visit / how many / did you _____

7. you like / which theme park / did / the most _____

8. you / go / on / did / the Spider-Man ride _____

H In pairs, ask and answer the questions in **G**. Use the answers from the audio or make new answers.

✓ GOAL CHECK Ask about a Trip

1. Work in pairs. Ask your partner to choose one of these types of trips:

- a vacation
- a long weekend or short break
- a day trip

2. Write 5 questions for your partner about his / her trip.

3. Take turns asking and answering the questions.

> Where did you go... ?

> Did you take... ?

> How long did... ?

> Did you like... ?

GOAL Talk about Your Weekend

Adjectives	Emphatic Adjectives
good nice	excellent outstanding magnificent amazing
bad	awful terrible horrible
interesting	fascinating
tiring	exhausting
dirty	filthy
clean	spotless
big	enormous huge

Language Expansion: Emphatic Adjectives

A Write two or three emphatic adjectives below each photo.

_____   _____

_____   _____

B Complete the text with emphatic adjectives.

We had an (1) _____ weekend in Rome! It's a (2) _____

city. There is so much to see: museums, churches, ruins. We stayed in

a (3) _____ hotel. Everything about it was perfect. It had a

(4) _____ swimming pool and very friendly people.

Grammar

Simple Past of *to be*	
Statement	I **was** exhausted.
Negative	The food **wasn't** great.
Information Questions	How **was** your weekend?
Yes / No Questions	**Were** the rooms expensive?
Short answers	No, they **weren't**.

C Complete the text with *was*, *were*, *wasn't*, or *weren't*.

It (1) _____was_____ an amazing weekend. My friend likes diving, so we

went out on his boat. There (2) _____ a lot of different fish, and

we saw a turtle. I wanted to see a shark, but there (3) _____ any.

It (4) _____ the wrong time of year. At night, we stayed at a cheap

hotel on an island. My bed (5) _____ very comfortable, but the

rooms (6) _____ spotless.

D Match the questions about the weekend in **C** to the correct answers.

1. How was your weekend? _____
2. Were there a lot of different fish? _____
3. Were there any sharks? _____
4. Where was your hotel? _____
5. Was your bed comfortable? _____
6. Were the rooms clean? _____

a. No, it wasn't.
b. It was great!
c. Yes, there were. And we saw a turtle.
d. Yes, they were.
e. It was on an island.
f. No, there weren't. It was the wrong time of year.

Conversation

E 🎧 34 Listen to the conversation. What was good about the weekend? What was bad?

Alex: How was your weekend?
Camilo: It was <u>good</u>. I went camping with Lee.
Alex: Really? How was the weather?
Camilo: It was <u>bad</u> on the first day. It rained non-stop!
Alex: Oh, no! What did you do?
Camilo: We went to a hotel, but there weren't any rooms. Then we found another hotel. It was more expensive, but the rooms were <u>clean</u> and the food was <u>good</u>.
Alex: So, did you go hiking?
Camilo: Yes, on the second day. It was sunny, so we hiked to a <u>big</u> cliff. It was <u>tiring</u>, but a lot of fun. The view from the top was <u>good</u>! Anyway, how was your weekend?
Alex: It was OK, but it was very boring compared to yours!

F Practice the conversation in pairs. Switch roles and practice again.

G Change the underlined adjectives to emphatic adjectives and practice again.

Cliffs at Zion National Park, Utah, United States

 GOAL CHECK
Talk about Your Weekend

1. Think about a recent weekend when you did something special. Make notes about what you did.
2. In pairs, ask and answer questions about your weekends.

SPEAKING STRATEGY

Asking about Your Weekend

How was your weekend / the weather / your hotel / the party?
What did you do?
Where was the hotel?
Who was there?
(It was) Great! / OK. / Not bad. / Boring.

D GOAL Describe an Ancient Place

Reading

A Look at the photo. Where do you think this is? Are there places like this in your country?

B Read the first paragraph. When did Hiram Bingham travel to Peru? Why did he go? What did he find?

C MY WORLD Do you know the names of any other explorers? What places did they explore?

D Read the article and answer the questions.

1. Did Bingham see ruins in Ollantaytambo?
2. How did he travel to Mandorpampa?
3. How much did he pay Arteaga?
4. Was the climb to Machu Picchu easy?
5. Where did they eat?
6. What did Bingham find on top of the mountain?
7. When did he return to Machu Picchu?
8. What did they clear?

E Match the words from the article to the definitions.

1. explore __f__
2. archaeologist ____
3. ancient ____
4. ruins ____
5. hut ____
6. clear ____

a. very old
b. a person who studies places from the past
c. a small house
d. cut down and take away
e. old buildings with parts falling down
f. travel somewhere to find new things

F In pairs, think of an ancient place you know about. Answer as many of the questions as you can.

1. What is it called?
2. Where is it?
3. What was it?
4. Who built it?
5. When did they build it?
6. Other facts?

✓ GOAL CHECK

Describe your ancient place to another pair.

The Cradle of the Inca Empire

*Most people travel to relax, but some people travel to explore new places. In 1911, an American archaeologist named Hiram Bingham traveled to Peru, where he was the first **foreigner** to see Machu Picchu, the lost city of the Incas. Read his report of the journey.*

In 1911, I went to Cuzco, in Peru, looking for ancient Inca ruins. We left Cuzco and traveled to the modern city of Urubamba. We then continued down the Urubamba River until we came to the beautiful little town of Ollantaytambo. We continued down the river, and six days after we left Cuzco, we arrived at a place called Mandorpampa. A man came and introduced himself as Arteaga, and I asked him about ruins. He told us of some ruins in the mountains, called Machu Picchu. I offered to pay him 50 cents per day to take us to the ruins, and he agreed.

The next day, we crossed the river and began an exhausting climb. At noon, we arrived at a little grass hut. The people there were very friendly and gave us some boiled potatoes and cool water. The view was magnificent, and the water was delicious, but there were no ruins. However, we continued upward until at last we arrived on top of the mountain. Immediately, we found some ancient Inca walls made of white stone. I knew at once that this was a truly amazing place.

I returned to Machu Picchu in 1912, and we began to clear the forest. We started to see the ruins, and they were outstanding. The walls are made from enormous stones, and as we continued to clear the forest, we discovered more and more ruins. At last, the lost city of Machu Picchu appeared before us.

foreigner someone from another country

E | GOAL Find and Share Information Online

Communication

A Before you travel to a new place, where can you find information about it?

B How often do you use the internet to look for information about these things? Write *never*, *sometimes*, or *often*.

- a travel destination _____
- events in your town or city _____
- the weather _____
- your favorite sports team _____

- shopping items _____
- your favorite celebrities _____
- the English language _____
- your family and friends _____

C In pairs, compare your answers in **B**. Discuss where you usually find the information.

On an app	In a book	On a blog
On social media	On a website	Other: _____

> I often look for information about the weather. I use an app called...

D Read three online texts. Where do you think they are from? Why?

1. A travel blog _____
2. A social media bio _____
3. A tourist website _____

A Hi! My name's Lydia and I was born in 1993. When I was a child, I loved reading books about travel. Between 2011 and 2014, I went to university and studied geography. When I finished university, I didn't know what to do next. So, a year later, I left England and started to travel around the world, and I'm still traveling!	**B** Two days ago, we left Bangkok and traveled north to the province of Chiang Rai. Yesterday, we walked 10 kilometers through the countryside and we didn't see any other tourists—it was amazing! In the evening, we ate dinner with a local family. They were so friendly.	**C** During the 17th and 18th century, the town became famous as a port, and many people sailed here from other countries. Last year, it celebrated its 500th birthday and local people had a big party in the streets with music and fireworks.

Writing

E Read the time references below. Then <u>underline</u> the time references in **D**.

WRITING SKILL: Time References		
Yesterday,	Between 2015 and 2017,	The day before
Last night / month / year,	In 2001,	yesterday,
This morning,	On January 1st,	When I was young /
A week / month / year ago,	During the 20th century,	a child / a student,

Complete the sentences with time references. Then compare them in pairs.

1. I learned to ride a bicycle _____.

2. _____ I went to the movies.

3. I took my first vacation _____.

4. My town (or city) was built _____.

✓ **GOAL CHECK** Find and Share Information Online

1. Choose one of the following and write a post about:

   • a vacation or trip you took. (for a travel blog)

   • you and your life. (for a social media bio)

   • the history of your town or city. (for a tourist website)

   Remember to use time references and the simple past.

2. Share your posts in pairs. Did your partner use time references and the simple past?

Wat Huay Pla Kung, Chiang Rai, Thailand

VIDEO JOURNAL

VIETNAM'S GREEN JEWELS

A Look at the photo. Why do you think this is a popular tourist destination?

B What makes a good tourist destination? Number the factors in order of importance. (1 = most important, 7 = least important) In a small group, compare your answers.

_____ Beautiful views

_____ Good hotels and restaurants

_____ Safety

_____ Stores and souvenir shops

_____ An international airport

_____ Tours and sightseeing with a guide

_____ Friendly local people

C Watch the video. Check ( ) the things the narrator talks about.

__✓__ 1. The location of the bay

_____ 2. Where tourists can stay

_____ 3. The legend of the dragon

_____ 4. The scientific history of the bay

_____ 5. The local food and drink

_____ 6. Different animals in the area

_____ 7. A future problem for the bay

The islands of Ha Long Bay in Vietnam

Read the sentences about the video. Match the underlined words to a–g.

1. It's one of Vietnam's most popular destinations. ____
2. Most of <u>them</u> are uninhabited by humans. ____
3. <u>It</u> breathed fire. <u>It</u> also breathed green jewels. ____
4. <u>They</u> are between 160 and 330 feet tall. ____
5. <u>One</u> is on an island, and <u>the other</u> is on the water. ____
6. <u>Half of them</u> are from overseas. ____

a. tourists
b. Ha Long Bay
c. karsts
d. two national parks
e. the islands
f. the dragon

E The narrator says: "Tourism is good for the local economy, but too many tourists is bad for the environment." Why is this?

F Work in groups. Choose a local tourist destination and plan your own video about it. Make notes about each part of your video in the table below and your notebooks.

Time	What can you see in the video?	What does the narrator say?
0–30 seconds		
30–60 seconds		
60–90 seconds		
90–120 seconds		

85

The New Zealand
rugby team does a
haka, a traditional
dance and chant,
before its games.

Look at the photo and answer the questions.

1 What are these people doing? How are they communicating?

2 In what ways do you communicate with your family and friends?

UNIT 7 GOALS

A. Talk about Personal Communication

B. Exchange Contact Information

C. Describe Characteristics and Qualities

D. Compare Types of Communication

E. Compare Formal and Informal Communication

87

GOAL Talk about Personal Communication

Vocabulary

A In groups, read the information about teenagers in the US. Which facts do you think are surprising? Not surprising?

How Teenagers Use Technology in the US

72% look at their smartphone as soon as they wake up.

85% share photos on social media.

100% who have a smartphone write text messages, making it the most popular feature.

78% use internet search engines to help with school work.

41% send their teachers emails.

45% use the internet almost all the time.

90% play video games on a computer or a game console.

61% watch TV shows on the internet, not on a traditional TV.

B Match the words in blue to the photos.

C Delete the one verb that cannot be used with the noun.

1. *share* / *take* / ~~*write*~~ a photo
2. *watch* / *text* / *turn on* the TV
3. *watch* / *send* / *check* text messages
4. *search* / *find* / *use* the internet
5. *play* / *download* / *read* video games
6. *buy* / *log on to* / *use* social media

D In pairs, write four sentences using the words in **C**.

I often share photos of my friends on social media.

> I often... photos of my friends on social media.

E Work with another pair. Read each of your sentences in **D**, but do not say the verb. Can the other pair guess the missing verb?

> Is it *share*?

> Yes, it is. Correct!

Grammar

Verbs with Direct and Indirect Objects

Subject	Verb	Indirect Object	Direct Object
I	sent	**Mike**	**a photo**.
Her parents	bought	**her**	**a smartphone**.
I	will give	**you**	**a call**.

F Read the sentences and match them to the structure (a or b).

a. Subject + verb + direct object

b. Subject + verb + indirect object + direct object

1. We use the internet.   _a_
2. I left you a voicemail.   ____
3. They send their friends photos.   ____
4. My sister plays video games.   ____
5. I didn't buy him a smartphone.   ____
6. My grandmother still mails me letters!   ____

G Unscramble the words to write sentences. <u>Underline</u> the direct objects.

1. sent / a / I / text message / Marco

   _____

2. gave / My / brother / a / me / video game

   _____

3. address / me / his / Find / email

   _____

4. new / Jim / a / smartphone / I / bought

   _____

5. a / your / mom / Give / call

   _____

 GOAL CHECK
Talk about Personal Communication

1. Look at the facts in **A** again. Which sentences are true for you? Rewrite the untrue sentences so they are true for you.

2. In pairs, use your answers in item 1 to tell your partner about how you communicate. Comment on your partner's answers.

> I never send my parents text messages. They use email.

> Mine, too. And I usually communicate with friends by social media.

B GOAL Exchange Contact Information

Listening

A 🎧 36 Listen and number a–c in the order you hear them.

a. a radio show _____   **b.** a conversation _____   **c.** a voicemail _____

B 🎧 36 Listen again and complete the missing information.

Conversation 1:

Joel's address: _____

Conversation 2:

Telephone number: _____

Text: _____

Social media handle: _____

Conversation 3:

Email: _____

Website: _____

C Below is the contact information of some famous places. Take turns reading each of them aloud in pairs.

1. Avenida Presidente Castelo Branco, Rio de Janeiro, 20271-130, Brazil. Tel. +55 800 062 7222 www.maracana.br email: info@maracana.br

2. 1600 Pennsylvania Ave. NW, Washington DC, 20500, US. Tel. 1 202 456 1111 www.whitehouse.gov email: comments@whitehouse.gov

3. 5 Avenue Anatole France, 75007, Paris, France. Tel. 33 08 92 70 12 39 www.tour-eiffel.fr

---

PRONUNCIATION: Sentence Stress for Clarification

Clarify numbers and spelling by stressing words or letters, like this:
That was 13, *not* 30. *One three.*
Is that P *as in* Paris *or* B *as in* Beijing?

D 🎧 37 Listen to these sentences and underline the stressed words or letters.

1. That's fif<u>teen</u>, not fif<u>ty</u>.

2. It's A as in apple.

3. It ends in dot org, not dot com.

4. Was that zero zero one or zero zero two?

5. Can you spell your last name?

E 🎧 37 Listen again and repeat. Stress the correct words.

Write your (or made up) contact information in the first column of the chart.

	Me	Classmate 1	Classmate 2	Classmate 3
Name				
Phone number				
Email address				
Mailing address				
Social media handle				

✓ **GOAL CHECK** Exchange Contact Information

Ask three of your classmates for their contact information. Complete the chart.

What's your email address?

My email address is...

In 2016, the opening ceremony for the Olympics was at Maracaña Stadium in Rio de Janeiro, Brazil.

GOAL Describe Characteristics and Qualities

Language Expansion: The Senses

A Look at the photos from different countries. Match the comments to the photos.

1. _____

2. _____

4. _____

3. _____

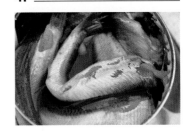

5. _____

    a. "That smells terrible!"   **d.** "It tastes delicious!"

    b. "He looks very old."   **e.** "This feels soft."

    c. "They sound fantastic!"

Grammar: Sensory Verbs

B Complete the table with these words.

ears	feels	looks	nose	smells	taste	touch

The Five Senses	Parts of the Body	Sensory Verbs
sight	eyes	5. _____
hearing	3. _____	sounds
1. _____	mouth and tongue	tastes
smell	4. _____	6. _____
2. _____	hands and fingers	7. _____
We use sensory verbs to describe the characteristics and qualities of people, animals, and things.		

C Underline the five sensory verbs in **A**. Then answer these questions.

    1. What verb form do you normally use with sensory verbs? _____

    2. What type of word usually follows a sensory verb? _____

D Write the sensory verbs in these sentences.

1. When I see people rock climbing, I think it _____ very dangerous!
2. Turn that music off! It _____ terrible!
3. I like your perfume. It _____ nice.
4. These french fries _____ too salty.
5. I prefer these shoes. They _____ more comfortable.

E In groups, say which sensory verb(s) can be used with each adjective. There may be more than one answer. Then say a new sentence with each adjective and a sensory verb.

beautiful	expensive	loud	polluted	sweet
cold	hard	noisy	smooth	tired

Conversation

F 🎧 38 Listen to the conversation. Which headphones does Susan prefer? Why?

Bill: What do you think of these headphones?
Susan: The black ones? They look <u>OK</u>.
Bill: Do they fit your head? Try them on.
Susan: I think they feel <u>too big</u>.
Bill: Yes, I agree. They look <u>huge</u>! What about those blue ones?
Susan: They look <u>very expensive</u>. But they feel <u>more comfortable</u>.
Bill: How do they sound? Listen to some music with them.
Susan: Wow! They sound <u>amazing</u>!

SPEAKING STRATEGY

Give Your Opinion
I think it looks / feels / sounds / tastes / smells...
What do you think about...?
I don't think it...
I agree. / I disagree.

G Practice the conversation in pairs. Switch roles and practice it again.

H Change the underlined words and make a new conversation.

✓ **GOAL CHECK**
Describe Characteristics and Qualities

My favorite dish is tacos. I think they taste amazing!

In pairs, take turns talking about the characteristics of four of the following. Then give your opinion about your partner's choices.

- Your favorite piece of technology
- Your favorite dish
- Your favorite type of music
- Your favorite perfume / aftershave
- Your favorite place for a vacation
- Your favorite celebrity

GOAL Compare Types of Communication

Reading

A Does each type of human communication use the sense of sight, hearing, touch, or more than one?

shaking hands	smiling	waving
writing	kissing	shaking your head
nodding your head	laughing	yelling

B Match these sentences to actions in **A**.

1. "I disagree with you."   **4.** "That's so funny!"

2. "I agree with you."   **5.** "Nice to meet you."

3. "I'm happy to see you."   **6.** "Goodbye."

C **MY WORLD** Do any of the examples of body language in **A** have a different meaning in your country? What are some examples of body language used in your country?

D Read the article. Match the words to the definitions.

_a_ **1.** body language   **a.** communication with the body

___ **2.** greet   **b.** feelings

___ **3.** emotions   **c.** do in a similar way

___ **4.** sense of humor   **d.** meet and say "hello"

___ **5.** copy   **e.** ability to have fun

E Are these actions done by humans, elephants, or both? Underline the supporting information in the article.

1. Speak with words and language   _humans_

2. Spread ears to show anger or aggression   ___

3. Shake their head to disagree   ___

4. Shake their head to show they are happy   ___

5. Touch each other to show their feelings   ___

6. Laugh   ___

7. Have a sense of humor   ___

8. Copy sounds they hear   ___

 GOAL CHECK

In groups, describe at least one similarity and one difference between the different types of communication in each pair.

- Human / Animal
- Face-to-face / Electronic
- Speaking / Writing
- Social media / Text

Do you speak "elephant"?

As humans, we communicate using the senses of sight, touch, and hearing. We send messages with body language, we greet friends with touch, and we speak using words to show our emotions and ideas. Animals don't communicate in as many ways as humans—for example, they don't have language like we do— but many animals do also use the senses of sight, touch, and hearing. A good example of this is elephant communication.

Like humans, elephants understand each other by looking at each other's body language. To send a message, they use their whole body, or individually their heads, eyes, mouth, ears, trunk, tail, or feet. For example, elephants spread their ears to show anger. And while humans shake their heads to disagree, elephants do this to show they are happy.

As with humans, touch is also very important between elephants. Just like a human mother holds her baby, a mother elephant regularly touches her young **calf** with her trunk. Elephants also show they are friendly when they touch other elephants. And when they want to have fun, they hold each other by the trunk and pull, like in this photo. Even if they can't laugh like a human, elephants have a great sense of humor.

Elephants have very large ears, which means they can hear other elephants from as far as 2.5 miles away. Like humans, they can also copy sounds and make their own sounds that seem to communicate basic human words and phrases like, "Hello," "I love you," and "Let's go."

So while it's true that humans are amazing at communication, elephants also communicate in ways that we can't, and that's probably true for other animals, too. The next time your **pet** dog or cat looks at you, touches you, or makes a noise, it's probably trying to tell you something very important!

calf young elephant
pet an animal in your house

GOAL Compare Formal and Informal Communication

Communication

A How often do you use each of the following? Every day, sometimes, or never?

email   letter   phone call   social media   text message

B Which types of communication in **A** would you use in each situation? Fill in the *Me* column.

You want to. . .	Me	My partner
1. send a photo to your grandparents.		
2. apply for a new job.		
3. keep in touch with friends from Brazil.		
4. send an assignment to your teacher.		
5. invite a friend out tonight.		

C Compare your answers in pairs. Fill in the information for your partner. Give reasons for your answers.

Writing

D Read the information below. Then discuss in pairs if you would use formal or informal writing for each situation in **B**.

WRITING SKILL: Formal and Informal Writing
With **formal writing** (often to people we don't know), we use full sentences and special expressions: *Dear Mr. Smith, I am writing to apply for the job of... Please see my attached resume.*   With **informal writing** (often to people we know well), we use shorter sentences and contracted forms. Sometimes we also leave words out.   *Hi! I'm having a party. Want to come?*

A family enjoys a ride at a theme park in Texas, US.

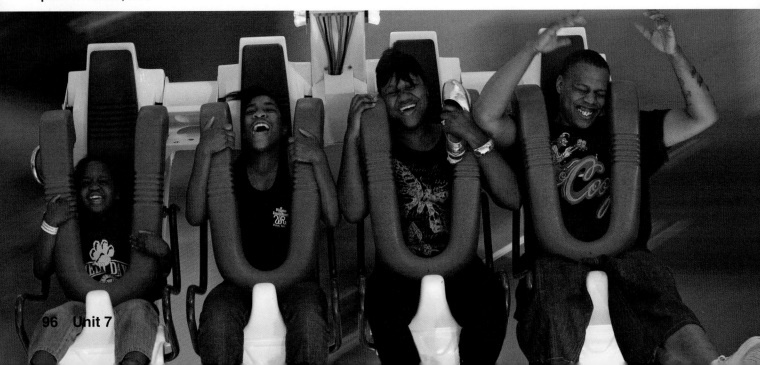

E In pairs, look at the three messages and number them from 1 to 3 (1 = most formal, 3 = least formal). Underline words and phrases that help you decide.

> Hi Chen,
> I'm having a party. It's my 18th birthday and my family and friends are meeting at a theme park. It'd be great to see you. The invitation is attached with the time, date, and address. Hope you can come!
> Best,
> Paula

> Dear Miss Jones:
> I am writing to request information about art courses at your college. I am a student in Argentina and I would like to study art in your country. Also, could you please send me information about accommodation and prices.
> Best regards,
> Paula Fratelli

> Hi! I'm at the theme park. Where r u?

F Match the formal and informal expressions with similar meanings.

1. Dear Miss Jones: ___f___

2. I would like... _____

3. I'd like to request... _____

4. Please see the attached photos. _____

5. I am writing to inform you... _____

6. I look forward to seeing you. _____

7. Thank you for inviting me. _____

8. Best regards, _____

a. I want

b. I'm writing to tell you...

c. See you soon.

d. Thanks for the invite!

e. Can I have... ?

f. Hi Jill!

g. Here are the photos.

h. Bye for now!

✓ GOAL CHECK
Compare Formal and Informal Communication

1. Write two emails.

- Write a short formal email (60–70 words) to a travel company. You want information about their vacations next summer. Ask for information about their hotels and prices.

- Write a short informal email (40–50 words) to a friend. You plan to have a party with family and friends for your parents' wedding anniversary. Invite him or her to the party.

2. Exchange emails with a partner. How well does your partner use formal and informal language? Give feedback.

A NEW VIEW OF THE MOON

Filmmaker Wylie Overstreet stands next to his telescope and looks at the moon.

A People often have similar feelings about these things. How do you feel when you...

- see the sun rise or set?
- smell bread in the oven?
- sit in a traffic jam for an hour?
- find a spider in your house?
- see the moon and stars at night?

B In groups, compare your answers in **A**. Did you all have the same feelings? Why?

C Watch the video. Number the things in the order you see them.

1 There is a view of Los Angeles.

☐ The man asks people if they want to look.

☐ The man takes his telescope outside.

☐ A woman says, "You can see the craters!"

☐ The man takes his telescope away.

☐ A man takes a photo of the moon.

☐ A boy tells his brother to look.

D These phrases show surprise. Check (✓) the phrases you hear in the video. Then watch again and check. As you watch, listen to the intonation.

1. No way! ☐
2. Isn't that awesome? ☐
3. That is so cool! ☐
4. What? ☐
5. Fantastic! ☐
6. I've never seen this before! ☐
7. Really? ☐
8. Isn't that amazing? ☐
9. That is incredible! ☐
10. Wow! ☐

E 🎧 40 Listen and repeat. Say the expressions in **D** with surprise and interest.

F Write down three pieces of surprising news to tell a partner. They can be true or untrue. Take turns saying your news and responding with phrases from **D**.

G Read the quote from the video. Do you agree? Why?

*"It makes you realize that we are all on a small little planet and we all have the same **reaction** to the universe we live in. I think there's something special about that. Something **unifying**. It's a great **reminder** that we should look up more often."*

reaction something you do in a situation
unifying bringing people together
reminder something that helps you remember

Making Plans

Look at the photo and answer the questions.

1 What do people at a wedding dream about for the future?

2 What is your dream for the future?

UNIT 8 GOALS

A. Talk about Plans

B. Plan a Project

C. Make Predictions

D. Solve a Problem

E. Describe Future Trends

It's a wedding party in Punta del Este, Uruguay. Family and friends push the brother of the bride into a pool.

GOAL Talk about Plans

Vocabulary

A Match the plans to the photos. Write the number.

1. buy a new car
2. buy my own house
3. clean the house
4. do the laundry
5. get a new job
6. get married
7. have children
8. speak English fluently
9. study for the next test
10. take a vacation

B Write the plans in **A** in the correct columns.

Short-term plans	Long-term plans

C Which of the short-term plans in **B** do you have? Discuss in pairs.

D Number the long-term plans in **B** in order of importance to you. (1 = most important). Then compare your lists in the same pairs.

Grammar

Future: *Be going to*		
Statements	We**'re going to buy** a new car tomorrow.	
Negative	He**'s not going to get** a new job next year.	
Yes / No Questions	**Are** you **going to do** the laundry this weekend?	Yes, I am. No, I'm not.
Wh- Questions	**When are** you **going to pay** the phone bill?	On Tuesday.

E 🎧 41 Complete this conversation with *be going to* and the verbs in parentheses. Then listen and check your answers.

REAL LANGUAGE

Say *Yes, I am,* or *No, I'm not* when you are certain. Say *I'm not sure* when you are not certain.

Kat: Hey! (1) _Are you going to come_ (you / come) to my party this weekend?

Ben: I'm not sure. I have a test on Monday, so I (2) _____ (study) for that all weekend.

Kat: Which test?

Ben: It's for my Mandarin class. My sister and I (3) _____ (take) a vacation to China next year, so I want to speak the language.

Kat: Wow! That's great. But my party is in the evening and it (4) _____ (be) fun! And you (5) _____ (not / study) all weekend. You (6) _____ (need) a break.

Ben: That's true. OK, see you on Saturday.

F What are your short-term and long-term plans? Check (✓) the correct column.

Short-term plans			
Are you going to ...	**Yes, I am.**	**I'm not sure.**	**No, I'm not.**
eat out tonight?			
go to a party tonight?			
play or watch a sport this weekend?			
rest this weekend?			

Long-term plans			
Are you going to ...	**Yes, I am.**	**I'm not sure.**	**No, I'm not.**
start your own business?			
learn another language?			
move to another country?			
buy a new car?			

G In pairs, ask and answer the questions in **F**. Then ask a *Wh-* question for each.

> Are you going to start your own business?

> Yes, I am.

> What type of business are you going to start?

> I'm not sure. Maybe a language school.

✓ **GOAL CHECK** Talk about Plans

> I'm going to take a vacation soon.

1. Write three of your short-term plans and three of your long-term plans.

2. In pairs, talk about your plans and ask each other more questions.

> Where are you going to go?

B **GOAL** Plan a Project

Listening

A Look at the photo. Answer the questions.

1. What do you think Molly Ferrill does?

2. What subject do you think she specializes in?

B 🎧 42 Listen to an interview with Molly. Check your answers in **A**.

C 🎧 42 Listen to the interview again. Complete the notes about Molly's next project. Use words from the interview.

What is the project?	When?	Are there other people?	Is there special equipment?
A _____ series about _____ wildlife protection officers and the species of _____ they protect.	**Start:** She's going to leave in _____. **Finish:** It's going to take _____.	She's going to work with other _____.	1. _____ 2. lenses 3. microphones 4. _____ _____

D 🎧 42 In pairs, compare your answers in **C**. Then listen again and check.

WORD FOCUS

wildlife protection officers people who keep animals safe

species types of animals

protect keep safe from danger

video series more than one video about the same subject

104 Unit 8

PRONUNCIATION: Reduced Form of *going to*

🎧 43 In natural speech, *going to* is often reduced to sound like *gonna*. The words are combined and the vowels also change. Listen to and repeat the sample sentences.
I'm going to buy a new computer.
Are you going to come?

E 🎧 44 Listen to the sentences and check (✓) the correct box.

	Full Form	Reduced Form
1. I'm going to make a video.		✓
2. Are you going to work with anyone else?	✓	
3. When are you going to leave?		
4. We're going to leave in two months.		
5. What special equipment are you going to need for the trip?		
6. We're going to pack different types of clothing.		
7. When are you going to finish the project?		

F In pairs, take turns reading the sentences in **E** with either the full form or the reduced form. Your partner has to say which form you used.

G In groups, plan one of these projects for your school:

- Create a website with information and news about your school and neighborhood.

- Make a short video called "A day in the life of a student."

- Plan an event to celebrate the end of the year.

 GOAL CHECK Plan a Project

1. In your groups, discuss each part of the project and write down information in the table.

What is the project?	When are you going to start and finish?	Who is going to do each part?	What are you going to need?

2. Present your plans for the project to the class or another group. Use *going to* in your presentation.

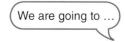

We are going to …   We are going to need …

GOAL Make Predictions

Language Expansion: Energy

A Look at the photo and read about Japan. Then answer the questions.

1. What does the photo show?

2. What type of energy will Japan use more in the future?

The Future of Energy in Japan

These are solar panels on the top of a building in Tokyo. Japan will use more renewable energy in the future.

coal	gas
oil	wave
wind	wood

B Write each type of energy from the box under the matching photo.

1. _____

2. _____

3. _____

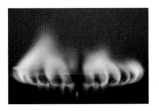

4. _____

5. _____

6. _____

C Write which types of energy in **A** and **B** are renewable and which are non-renewable.

Renewable Energy	Non-renewable Energy

D **MY WORLD** What types of energy does your country use at the moment?

Grammar

Future: *Will*		
Statements	Japan **will** use more solar energy in the future.	
Negative	It **won't** use non-renewable energy.	
Questions	**Will** it use renewable energy?	Yes, it **will**. / No, it **won't**.
You can use both **will** and **be going to** to talk about future predictions. *It **won't use*** oil. / *It **isn't going to use*** oil.		

E Put the words in the correct order.

1. will / my country / use / wind power _____.

2. cars / use / won't / gas _____.

3. speak / English / most people / will _____.

4. live / people / won't / on the Moon _____.

Conversation

F 🎧 45 Listen to a conversation between two people from Japan and Scotland.

Rika: I don't think we will use as much non-renewable energy in the next five years, so we'll need lots of <u>solar energy</u>. What about in <u>Scotland</u>? Will you use new types of energy?

Alex: Yes, we will. But we probably won't use a lot of <u>solar energy</u>.

Rika: Will you use <u>wind power</u>?

Alex: Yes, we will. And maybe we'll also use <u>wave energy</u>.

Rika: What's <u>wave energy</u>?

Alex: It's <u>energy from waves in the ocean</u>.

Rika: Wow! That's great.

SPEAKING STRATEGY

Opinions about the Future
I (don't) think we will ...
Maybe we will / won't ...

G In pairs, change the underlined words and make new conversations about your country.

 GOAL CHECK Make Predictions

1. Read the questions and write two more in the chart. Check (✓) your answers.

	Me			Partner		
In the future, do you think ...	**Yes**	**Maybe**	**No**	**Yes**	**Maybe**	**No**
1. most houses will have solar panels?						
2. people will live under the sea?						
3. there will be enough food for everyone?						
4. summers will be hotter than now?						
5. people will travel to Mars?						
6.						
7.						

2. Ask a partner the questions and check (✓) his or her answers. Then compare your answers.

D GOAL Solve a Problem

Reading

A Look at the photo. What do you think this person does?

B Read the article and answer the questions.

1. What problem do some people in Myanmar have?

2. What is the solution?

C **MY WORLD** What is a problem in your town or city? What is the solution?

D Read the article again. Circle **T** for *true* or **F** for *false*.

1. The writer thinks that most people use electricity.   **T   F**

2. 1.1 billion people in the world have electricity.   **T   F**

3. Candles are not cheap and not safe in Myanmar.   **T   F**

4. The energy for the solar panels comes from the sun.   **T   F**

5. Rubén Salgado Escudero is from Myanmar.   **T   F**

6. Some villages will have larger solar panels in the future.   **T   F**

E Find these sentences in the third paragraph. Write the phrases for giving reasons.

1. Fishermen went fishing before sunrise _____ the solar panels.

2. Children could do their homework _____ electricity.

F Make sentences about solutions and results with the linking phrases in **E**.

1. There is less pollution / electric cars
   There is less pollution because of electric cars.

2. People have jobs / the new office building
   _____

3. The new park / local people have a place to relax
   _____

4. More people bike to work and school / new bike paths
   _____

✓ GOAL CHECK

1. In groups, imagine you have these problems in your town or city. Make a list of solutions for each.

   • A lot of people don't recycle plastic bottles.

   • Everyone drives to work, so the traffic is bad.

   • Lots of young people don't have jobs.

   • There's nowhere for people to relax downtown.

2. Present your solutions to the class. Tell them what you are going to do about each problem and why.

> We are going to build a new park.

> Because of the new park, people will have a place to relax.

In this photo by Rubén Salgado Escudero, a fisherman in Myanmar holds a solar panel and light.

Electricity from the Sun

When you go home this evening after school or after work, what is the first thing you are going to do? You're probably going to switch a light on, turn the heat or air conditioning on, and cook dinner or watch TV. Whatever you plan to do, you're probably going to use electricity.

Most of us use electricity without thinking about it, but approximately 1.1 billion people in the world don't have electricity. For example, in Myanmar, only 26% of the population has electricity. Outside of the cities, people get light from the sun during the day and from candles at night. Candles are expensive and dangerous, but now there is a safer and cheaper solution to this problem: small solar panels are easy to use and can give electricity immediately.

When Spanish photographer Rubén Salgado Escudero first visited Myanmar, he says: "I worked in villages and the people had no light at night. Then, one day, I visited a village with solar lights and people's everyday life was much easier. For example, fishermen went fishing before sunrise because of the solar panels. Children could do their homework as a result of electricity."

After his first visit, Rubén showed his photographs of people with their solar lights and he **raised money** to pay for more solar lights. Now, more people in Myanmar have solar panels; these panels take energy from the sun and then provide 12 hours of light during the night. In the future, Myanmar is going to build larger solar panels for some of these villages, but—for now—the smaller panels will continue to change people's lives.

raise money to ask for and receive money for a special purpose

E GOAL Describe Future Trends

Communication

A Take the personality test. Are you optimistic or pessimistic? What do the results say?

WORD FOCUS

An **optimistic** person thinks everything will be good in the future. A **pessimistic** person thinks that things will be bad in the future.

1. I _____ have a healthy and happy life.

   a. 'll certainly   **b.** 'll probably   **c.** probably won't

2. I _____ live to be 100 years old.

   a. 'll definitely   **b.** 'll possibly   **c.** definitely won't

3. I _____ have my dream job someday!

   a. 'll definitely   **b.** 'll possibly   **c.** definitely won't

4. I _____ speak perfect English one day!

   a. 'll definitely   **b.** 'll probably   **c.** probably won't

Results:

Count 3 points for each *a*, 2 points for each *b*, and 1 point for each *c*.

10–12: You are optimistic. ☺

4–6: You are pessimistic. ☹

7–9: You are in the middle. 😐

REAL LANGUAGE

We often use adverbs of certainty with *will*.
I'll **certainly** / **definitely** / **probably** / **possibly** *live to 100.*
A: *Will you have a happy life?*
B: *Yes,* **definitely***!*

B Change the four sentences in the quiz into questions. Write them in your notebook.

C In pairs, ask and answer the questions. Find out if your partner is optimistic or pessimistic.

Writing

D Read about future trends and answer the questions. Then fill in the charts.

> The population of the world is over 7 billion now, and this will definitely increase to 9 billion by 2050. Most of these people will live in cities. At the moment, 55% of people live in cities. In the future, this will probably go up to 70%, and the number of people in the countryside will decrease to 30%.

1. What will increase? What will decrease?

2. How certain is the writer about the predictions?

Where will we live?

THE PRESENT: 7 billion people

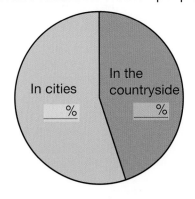

THE YEAR 2050: 9 billion people

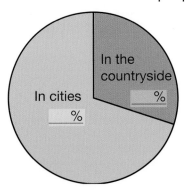

WRITING SKILL: Describing Trends

↑ increase / go up	It <u>will increase</u> **to** 9 billion **by** 2050. In the future, this <u>will probably go up</u> **to** 70%.
↓ decrease / go down	The number of people in the countryside <u>will decrease</u> **to** 30%.

 Look at the chart. Then complete the description of non-renewable energy in the future.

Global Non-renewable Energy

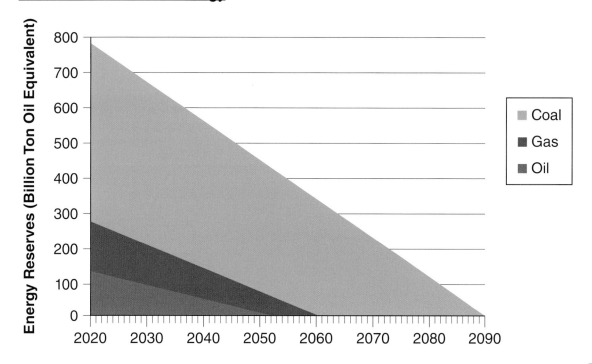

We probably (1) ___won't___ have any coal, gas, or oil (2) _____ 2090. At the moment, we have about 150 billion tons of oil, but we (3) _____ use all of it by 2052. By 2030, gas will (4) _____ about 200 billion. We still have a lot of coal in the world, but it will (5) _____, and by 2090 we (6) _____ won't have any coal left.

by
decrease
go down to
probably
will
~~won't~~

✓ GOAL CHECK
Describe Future Trends

Look at the information about what classes students take and write a description of the future trends. Use the paragraph in **E** as a model. Share your description in pairs. Then discuss if you think these trends are true for your city.

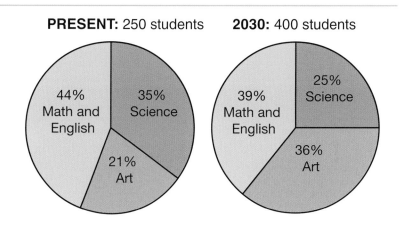

PRESENT: 250 students   **2030:** 400 students

A VIRTUAL CHOIR 2,000 VOICES STRONG

A MY WORLD In pairs, ask and answer the questions about music.

1. Who is your favorite musician?
2. Are you a fan of other musicians?
3. Do you ever sing? If yes, is it with a choir?
4. Do you play a musical instrument? If yes, which one?

B Watch the TED Talk. Number the stages of the project in the order Eric talks about them.

<u>1</u> One day, Eric watched a video of a girl singing his music. It gave him an idea.

___ Eric posted a piano track so the singers could hear the music.

___ Scott Haines edited all the videos together.

___ Eric recorded a track of himself conducting the music to the song "Lux Aurumque."

___ Singers started uploading their videos.

___ On Eric's blog, he asked singers to record videos of themselves singing his music.

<u>7</u> Eric posted the virtual choir video online.

C Watch the video again. Match the people to a–f.

1. A friend of Eric ___
2. Britlin Losee ___
3. Scott Haines ___
4. Melody Myers ___
5. Eric ___

a. She said, "I'm a little nervous!"
b. He said, "This is the project I've been looking for my whole life."
c. He said, "You have got to see this!"
d. He said, "I'll stop it there."
e. The winner of the soprano solo contest

D Complete the sentences about the video.

connect	download	link
post	upload	virtual

1. A _____ choir is a group of singers connected by the internet.
2. A friend emailed Eric a _____ to a YouTube video.
3. Eric wanted other singers to _____ their videos to YouTube.
4. The singers could _____ the music for free.
5. After the singers recorded their voices, they started to _____ their videos.
6. Eric thinks that technology and music can _____ people from around the world.

E Conductors usually work in person, but Eric conducts the choir online. In groups, think of a job and discuss if it is possible to do it online.

F Do you like to do the following things *online, in person*, or *both*? Add an idea of your own.

1. Play games	Online	In person	Both
2. Take classes	Online	In person	Both
3. Talk to family	Online	In person	Both
4. Go shopping	Online	In person	Both
5. Explore the world	Online	In person	Both
6. _____	Online	In person	Both

G Interview a classmate about what he or she prefers in **F**. Ask them to explain why. For the things they do online, ask them to explain how they do them.

ERIC WHITACRE

Composer, Conductor

Eric Whitacre's IDEA WORTH SPREADING
is that technology and music can connect
us in wonderful, unexpected ways. Watch
Whitacre's full TED Talk on TED.com

Types of Clothing

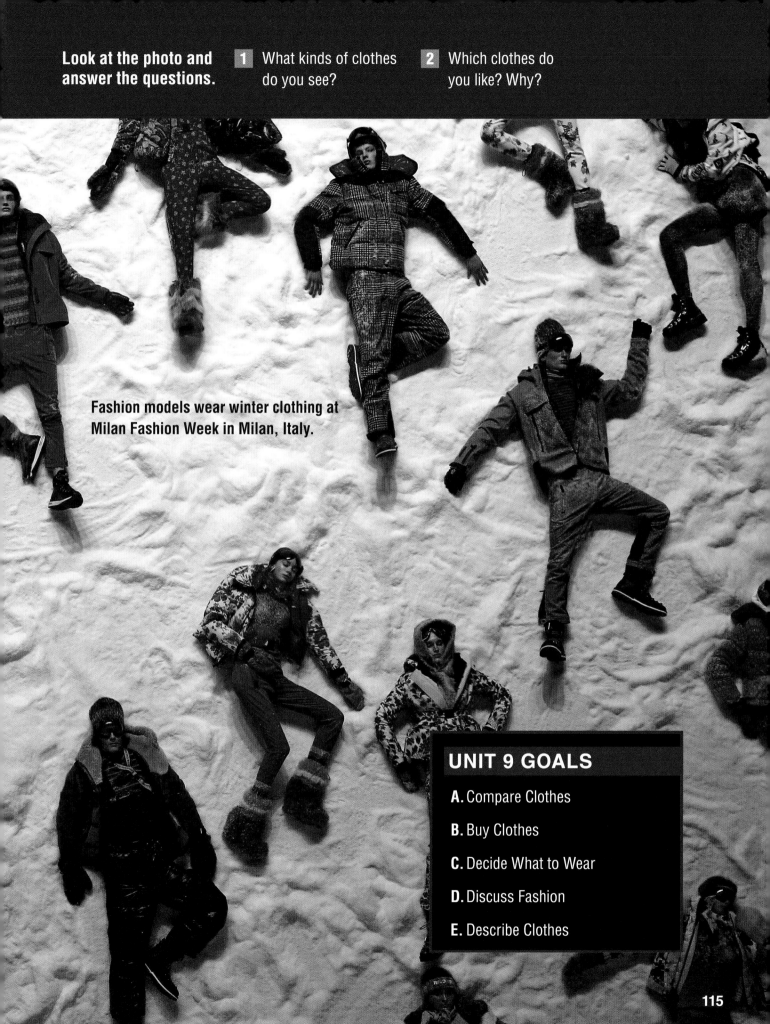

Look at the photo and answer the questions.

1 What kinds of clothes do you see?

2 Which clothes do you like? Why?

Fashion models wear winter clothing at Milan Fashion Week in Milan, Italy.

UNIT 9 GOALS

A. Compare Clothes

B. Buy Clothes

C. Decide What to Wear

D. Discuss Fashion

E. Describe Clothes

A GOAL Compare Clothes

Vocabulary

belt
blouse
cap
coat
gloves
handbag
hat
jacket
jeans
pants
shirt
shoes
skirt
sneakers
socks
suit
tie
T-shirt

A In pairs, label the pictures with words from the box.

B You can use these adjectives to describe clothes. Match the opposites.

1. beautiful _____   a. expensive
2. cheap _____   b. ugly
3. stylish, trendy _____   c. casual
4. light _____   d. old-fashioned
5. formal _____   e. tight
6. loose, comfortable _____   f. heavy

C Complete the sentences with adjectives from **B**. You can use more than one adjective for some sentences.

1. It's going to be cold tomorrow. You should bring a warm, _____ sweater or a jacket.
2. You can't wear those _____ jeans to a job interview!
3. That's a very _____ handbag! Where did you buy it?
4. I work in a law office, so I always wear something _____ when I meet clients, like a suit.

D Ask and answer these questions in pairs.

1. What adjectives describe the clothes in the picture in **A**?
2. What clothes are you wearing today? What adjectives describe them?
3. What types of clothes do you wear for special occasions? For example, a job interview or a family party?

Grammar

Comparatives		
Adjectives with one syllable Add *-er*.	cheap	Machine-made hats are **cheaper than** handmade hats.
Adjectives that end in -y Change the *-y* to *i* and add *-er*.	pretty	I like that dress, but this one is **prettier**.
Adjectives with two or more syllables Use *more* or *less* before the adjective.	beautiful	Eleanor is **more beautiful than** Eva.
	formal	These suits are **less formal than** those.
Irregular comparatives	good	Shopping in a store is **better than** shopping online.
	bad	My grades are **worse than** yours.
*The comparative form is often followed by *than*. *Use *much* to make a comparison stronger: *This coat is **much better than** the other one*.		

E Complete the sentences. Use the comparative form of the adjective in parentheses.

1. I like the green handbag, but it is _____ (expensive) than the brown one.

2. These jeans are _____ (nice) than my old ones.

3. These are stylish, but those black shoes are _____ (good) for work.

4. This sweater is ok, but I need a _____ (warm) one for the winter.

5. I think the blue blouse is _____ (pretty) than the black one.

F 🎧 47 Listen and read the conversation. Write in the missing comparative forms.

Danny: Can you help me? I have a job interview tomorrow and I don't know what to wear.

Edris: Sure. This brown jacket is nice.

Danny: Yes, but this black suit is (1) _____. And it matches my shirt.

Edris: Perfect! That's much (2) _____. Do you have a tie?

Danny: I only have two. Black or blue?

Edris: The blue tie is (3) _____. What about shoes?

Danny: Well, I like these brown shoes, but my black ones are (4) _____.

G Practice the conversation in pairs. Switch roles and practice again.

H Create and practice a new conversation comparing clothes. Start the conversation with: *Can you help me? I have a party tomorrow and I don't know what to wear.*

 GOAL CHECK Compare Clothes

In pairs, say sentences using comparative adjectives to compare the clothes:

- you and your partner are wearing today.
- your mother or father usually wear with what you usually wear.
- you are wearing today and the clothes you wore yesterday.
- you wear for school or work and the clothes you wear on weekends.

> Your shoes look more comfortable than mine.

> My father wears more old-fashioned clothes.

GOAL Buy Clothes

Listening

A 🎧 48 Listen to a conversation in a clothing store. What is the man buying? What color does he choose?

B 🎧 48 Listen again and answer the questions.

1. Does he want formal or casual shoes?
2. How many pairs of shoes does the man try on?
3. What size shoes does the man usually wear?
4. What size does he choose?
5. How much are the brown shoes?
6. How much are the white shoes?
7. Does he pay with cash or by card?

PRONUNCIATION: Stressed and Weak Syllables

In spoken English, some syllables are stressed and some are weak. Weak syllables usually do not sound as loud as stressed ones. The vowels are also usually longer in stressed syllables.

C 🎧 49 Listen and underline the stressed syllables in these sentences.

1. The skirt is cheaper than the shirt.
2. The blue tie is nicer than the black one.
3. Do you have a bigger size?
4. These ones are smaller than those.
5. This store is better.
6. The white shoes are more expensive than the brown ones.

Casual shoes for everyday wear or sports are often called *sneakers*.

D 🎧 49 Listen again and repeat the sentences in **C**.

Communication

E Who said the questions and statements below? Write S (salesperson) or C (customer).

1. Can I help you? _S_
2. I'd like to buy some blue shoes. _C_
3. Do you have anything less formal? ____
4. Can I try them on? ____
5. What size are you? ____
6. Do you have a bigger size? ____
7. Are they better? ____
8. How much are they? ____
9. Do you have anything less expensive? ____
10. What about these brown ones? ____
11. I'll take the blue ones. ____
12. Are you paying with cash or card? ____

F 🎧 48 Listen again and check your answers.

SPEAKING STRATEGY

Shopping
May / Can I help you?
May / Can I try ...?
What about ...?
I'll take ...

✓ GOAL CHECK Buy Clothes

1. Look at the flowchart. You're going to make a new conversation. Decide:
   - what the salesperson should say for each situation in a blue diamond.
   - what the customer should say for each situation in a green square.

   Follow the steps below and use phrases from **E** or your own ideas.

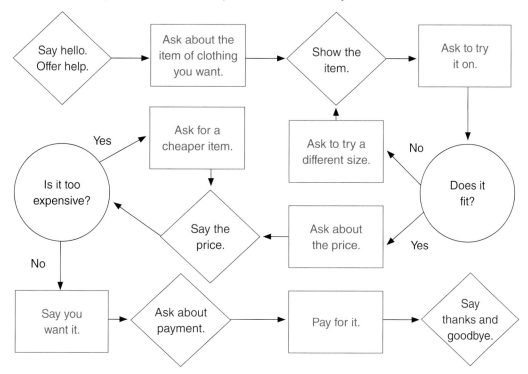

2. Practice the conversation using the flowchart. Take turns being the salesperson and the customer. Repeat the conversation with different items of clothing.

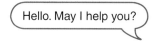

Hello. May I help you?

Yes, I'd like to buy a shirt.

C GOAL Decide What to Wear

This woman's dress is made from tree bark.

WORD FOCUS

synthetic materials
polyester, nylon, etc.
natural materials
cotton, wool, etc.

REAL LANGUAGE

My shirt is **made in** Italy.
(*made in* + a country)
It's **made from** cotton.
(*made from* + material)

Language Expansion: Clothing Materials

A Read the article and answer the questions.

1. What material do the women use to make clothes?

2. What type of clothing do people make with the material?

3. Is your country famous for a type of clothing? What is it made from?

Traditional Material for Modern Clothes

In the town of Masaka, Uganda, women make clothing materials from tree bark (the outer layer of a tree). Local people wear the clothes for special occasions and, now, modern clothing designers are starting to make fashionable clothes from the material.

B Label the clothing materials.

cotton	leather	silk	synthetic	wool

1. _____

2. _____

3. _____

4. _____

5. _____

C Which of these clothes are usually made from the materials in **B**? You can say more than one material.

gloves	handbags	jeans	pants
shirts	shoes	socks	ties

D **MY WORLD** Think about some of the clothes you are wearing today. What country are they made in? What material are they made from?

Grammar

Superlatives		
Adjectives with one syllable Add -est.	cheap	Polyester is **the cheapest** material.
Adjectives that end in -y Change the -y to i and add -est.	heavy	Leather is **the heaviest** material.
Adjectives with three or more syllables Use most before the adjective.	comfortable	I think silk is **the most comfortable** material.
Irregular superlatives	good bad	Wool is **the best** material for winter clothes. But it's **the worst** in the summer because it's so hot!

E Complete the sentences. Use the superlative form of the adjective in parentheses.

1. The _____ (strong) belts are made from leather.

2. Which jacket is the _____ (warm)? The brown one, the red one, or the black one?

3. This store sells the _____ (traditional) suits for men.

4. These Italian shirts are made from the _____ (good) cotton in the world.

F Write a sentence in your notebook for each of the pairs of adjectives in the box.

Wool is usually more expensive than cotton, but silk is the most expensive material.

	price	weight	warmth	texture
silk	++++	+	++	++++
wool	+++	++++	++++	+
cotton	++	+++	+++	+++
synthetic fiber	+	++	++	++

cheap / expensive
light / heavy
warm / cool
rough / smooth

Conversation

G 🎧 50 Listen to two friends plan a weekend. What is Lindsay going to take?

Pablo: I don't know what to pack. What are you going to take?

Lindsay: Two T-shirts, some shorts, and my leather boots. Oh, and a pair of wool socks to wear when I'm hiking.

Pablo: Is that all?

Lindsay: I'm also going to bring a warm sweater for the evenings.

Pablo: Is that everything? I think it's going to rain on Saturday night.

Lindsay: Is it? Maybe I should take my raincoat as well.

SPEAKING STRATEGY

Checking and Suggesting
Is that all?
What about ...?
Is that everything?
What else?

H Practice the conversation in pairs. Switch roles and practice it again.

✓ GOAL CHECK Decide What to Wear

1. In small groups, choose one way to spend a weekend together.

2. Discuss which items of clothing you are going to take with you. You can only take six items each. Talk about the clothes and say why you are taking them.

in a city with a great nightlife
camping in the summer
by the ocean in the winter

D GOAL Discuss Fashion

Reading

A Look at the photo. Which country do you think the woman is from? What is she wearing?

B Read the article. Check your predictions in **A** and match the titles to paragraphs 1–3.

  a. The modern lives of the "cholitas" _____

  b. Women with a special style of clothing _____

  c. International "chola" fashion _____

C Read the article again. Answer these questions.

  1. What was difficult for these women in the past? How are their lives different today?

  2. Why did Delphine Blast photograph some of the women?

  3. In which countries do people wear Eliana's clothes?

  4. Where did she show her clothes recently?

D Match the words in bold to the definitions.

  1. You might see women wearing **unique** clothing. _____

  2. This is the **fashion** of Aymaran women. _____

  3. She loved the **style** of the "cholitas" in the street. _____

  4. Many women ... want to wear these **outfits**. _____

  a. popular type of clothes

  b. sets of clothing (e.g., for a special occasion)

  c. very different from others

  d. a way of doing something (e.g., wearing certain clothes)

✓ GOAL CHECK

1. Do you agree or disagree with each statement? Why? Write notes in your notebook.

  1. Bowler hats are popular in my country.

  2. People with stylish clothes are always rich.

  3. School uniforms are a good idea.

  4. Stylish shoes are better than comfortable ones.

  5. Men should always wear suits to work.

  6. Women spend more money on clothes than men.

  7. Fashion in the 20th century was better than it is now.

  8. Most people like shopping for clothes.

2. In groups, discuss the statements. Give your opinions with reasons for your answers.

Pride Through Fashion

1   If you visit the Andes regions of Bolivia, Peru, or Chile, you might see women wearing unique clothing: bowler hats on top of their long black hair, handmade shawls, colorful blouses and skirts, and lots of jewelry. This is the fashion of Aymaran women. The Aymara are an **indigenous** group of people from the Andes mountains and Aymaran women's clothing is very different from any others. Locally, these women are called "cholitas" with their "chola" fashion.

2   In the past, it was difficult for Aymaran women to get good jobs or an education. They often lived in poorer parts of the cities. But in modern Bolivia, this is changing. More and more Aymaran women go to school and college. They often get well-paid jobs, so they now have money to spend on more expensive clothes. When French photographer Delphine Blast visited La Paz, the capital of Bolivia, she loved the style of the cholitas in the street, so she photographed some of these fashionably-dressed women.

3   Eliana Paco Paredes is an Aymaran fashion designer, and she says that chola clothes are in fashion at the moment, both in Bolivia and in other countries. She has a store in La Paz and sells the clothes to local people, and also internationally. "We dress many people in Peru, Argentina, Chile, Brazil, and some products we make go to Spain and Italy." Recently, Eliana showed her clothes at New York's Fashion Week, where they were very popular. "We're getting people to learn about what this clothing is, ... and many women outside of Bolivia want to wear these outfits." The popularity of the clothes is very satisfying for Eliana because it's good for her business, but it's also important because being "chola" now comes with a lot of **pride**.

indigenous people who were in a country before anyone else
pride a feeling of satisfaction from achievements, qualities, or possessions

GOAL Describe Clothes

Communication

A Discuss the questions as a class.

1. Do you normally buy clothes in a store or online?

2. Are there other items that you normally buy online? For example, books, technology, or food? Why?

B In pairs, write four sentences comparing shopping online with shopping in a store. Use these adjectives in the comparative form.

1. safe _____

2. quick _____

3. cheap _____

4. easy _____

C In pairs, discuss where these people should shop (online or in a store) and why. Then present your answers to the class and give your reasons.

	Online	In store
1. Jenny needs a new dress for her birthday party tonight.		
2. Hamadi lives in a small village, a long way from the city.		
3. Kenji isn't sure which smartphone to buy.		
4. Albert is 85 years old and can't walk very far.		
5. Rosa doesn't have a credit card.		
6. Mario hates waiting in line.		

Writing

D These ads are from an app where people can buy and sell clothes. Do you ever use apps like this?

Beautiful, gray and blue, wool sweater. It was made in Italy, and it's so soft and warm! I'm a size 8–10, so it would fit anyone around that size.
Price $15

Large, new swimsuit. I bought it last summer in Mexico, but I never wore it! It is made out of nylon.
Price $13

Comfortable, gray sneakers in great condition! They're perfect for everyday wear and they're very fashionable.
Price $11

E Read the ads. Check (✓) the information that is in each one.

	Sweater	Swimsuit	Sneakers
1. The seller's opinion	☐	☐	☐
2. Size	☐	☐	☐
3. Age	☐	☐	☐
4. Color	☐	☐	☐
5. Where it was made	☐	☐	☐
6. Material	☐	☐	☐

REAL LANGUAGE

We often give our opinion using adjectives:
I have a **beautiful** *sweater.* = **In my opinion**, *the sweater is beautiful.*

WRITING SKILLS: Describing Objects, Adjective Order, and Punctuation

Describing Objects

When you describe objects, such as clothes, you can use these phrases:

It's / They're made in (Italy).   It's / They're perfect for (jogging).   It's / They're so / very (comfortable).

Adjective Order

When you use more than one adjective before the object, use this order (from left to right):

Opinion	Size	Age	Color	Nationality	Material	Object
beautiful			black	Italian		sweater
	large	new			cotton	shorts
comfortable			blue and white			sneakers

Punctuation

Use commas between the adjectives: *It's a beautiful, black, Italian sweater.*

F Put the adjectives in the clothing ads in the correct order.

1. For sale! A (*black / warm / wool*) _____ hat. It's perfect for the winter.

2. I bought this (*Italian / stylish*) _____ suit 6 months ago and I wore it once!

3. I have two (*leather / brown / new*) _____ handbags. Buy 1 for $25 or 2 for $40!

4. (*Indonesian / silk / high-quality*) _____ ties in different colors. For every well-dressed man.

5. Buy now! Five pairs of (*cotton / red and green*) _____ children's socks.

✓ **GOAL CHECK** Describe Clothes

1. Write three ads to sell items of clothing or other objects (e.g., a bicycle, phone, etc.).

2. Put your ads around the classroom and read what your classmates want to sell. Check that they have written their adjectives in the correct order.

VIDEO JOURNAL

HOW YOUR T-SHIRT CAN MAKE A DIFFERENCE

A How many cups of coffee do you drink a day? How much water do you think you use when you drink your coffee?

B Complete the passage using the words from the Word Focus below. Does the information surprise you? Why?

It takes about 37 gallons of water to make a cup of coffee. The farmer uses water to grow the coffee. Then water is used to (1) _____ the coffee in a factory and also to (2) _____ the coffee to you. It also takes (3) _____ to make your cup of coffee: gas on the farm and electricity in the factory. This puts carbon into the air, which is called a (4) _____. One cup of coffee puts more than 3.5 ounces of carbon into the atmosphere.

> 1 gallon = 3.8 liters
> 1 liter = .26 gallons

WORD FOCUS

carbon footprint the amount of carbon a person uses
energy power from electricity, coal, gas, etc.
manufacture make something
transport move things from one place to another

C Watch the video. Complete the sentences.

40	1
~~2,700~~	70
97	900
1/3	

1. It takes __2,700__ liters of water to make one T-shirt.

2. 2,700 liters of water is enough for one person to drink for _____ days.

3. You use _____ gallons of water for one load of laundry.

4. _____% of water on Earth is salty.

5. Humans can only use _____% of the world's water.

6. _____% of that water grows crops.

7. You can save _____ of your T-shirt's carbon footprint.

D Watch the video again and complete the sentences.

1. Cotton is everywhere. It's in your furniture, _____, wallet, and your _____.

2. There are four ways your cotton T-shirt uses energy: to _____, to manufacture, to _____, and to care for it.

3. Use less water and _____: Skip the drying and _____.

E Ask and answer these questions in pairs.

1. How many T-shirts do you have?

2. How many T-shirts do you need?

3. Which T-shirt is your favorite?

4. How often do you wash your T-shirt in a washing machine? Do you always need to?

5. How often do you dry your T-shirt in a dryer? Do you always need to?

6. In the future, can you skip drying and ironing T-shirts?

F Work in groups. There are many ways to use fewer natural resources and have a smaller carbon footprint. Discuss the different ways you can do this with:

- shopping.
- products and packaging.
- food and drinks.
- transportation and travel.

Afterward, present your ideas to the class.

> We think people should ride bicycles more.

> We shouldn't use plastic bags for shopping.

Cotton grows on a cliff in Donegal, Ireland.

127

People paddleboarding
above a reef in Tonga in the
South Pacific

Look at the photo and answer the questions.

1 What are these people doing? Would you do this activity?

2 What other healthy activities can you do in the water?

UNIT 10 GOALS

A. Give Advice about Healthy Habits

B. Compare Lifestyles

C. Ask about Happiness

D. Discuss the Importance of Sleep

E. Explain Healthy Activities

GOAL Give Advice about Healthy Habits

Vocabulary

Noura has a **healthy** lifestyle. She's in **good shape** because she **works out** at the gym and rides her bike to school every day. She eats **healthy food**, like fresh fruit and vegetables.

Robert doesn't have a good **lifestyle**. He's in **bad shape** because he never gets any exercise. He eats too much **junk food** and no fruit or vegetables, so he gets sick a lot.

A Complete the sentences with the words in blue.

1. I need to exercise more. I'm _____ .

2. Helen doesn't have a _____ diet. She eats a lot of junk food.

3. I have a healthy _____ . I don't smoke and I get regular exercise.

4. I need to change my diet. I eat too much _____ .

5. Jane is feeling much healthier. She _____ and eats healthy food, like vegetables and fruit. Soon she'll be _____ .

B Are these activities healthy or unhealthy? Write the numbers for the activities in the chart below.

1. ~~Ride a bike to work~~
2. ~~Smoke~~
3. Watch lots of TV
4. Drink lots of water
5. Get 8 hours of sleep every night

6. Sunbathe all day
7. Eat lots of fruit and vegetables
8. Drink lots of coffee
9. Take the stairs
10. Work very long hours

Healthy	Unhealthy
1,	2,

C In groups, think of two more examples of healthy activities and two more examples of unhealthy activities. Write them in the chart and compare with the class.

Grammar

Modals: (*could, should, must*); *have to*		
Make Suggestions	Give Advice	Express Obligations
You **could** stop smoking.	You **should** stop smoking. You **shouldn't** add extra sugar.	You **must** stop smoking. You **have to** exercise more.
! gentle advice	!! strong advice	!!! very strong advice

D Write advice for the following situations. Then tell a partner your advice.

1. Tell your sister to stop smoking. !!! _____
2. Tell your father to go on a diet. !! _____
3. Tell your friend to stop watching so much TV. ! _____
4. Tell your brother to get more exercise. !! _____
5. Tell your mother to get more sleep. ! _____

E Write the advice you would give to these people in your notebook. Then compare your advice in pairs. Discuss any differences.

1. Aisha wants to lose weight.
2. Yun wants to be on the swim team.
3. Arata works too much.
4. Jaime needs some money.
5. Jack isn't happy at work.
6. Sam wants to get better grades.

Conversation

F 🎧 52 Listen to the conversation. What advice does Faisal give? How strong is it?

Alex: I feel so tired all the time. I don't have any energy. What should I do?
Faisal: Do you get eight hours of sleep every night?
Alex: Yes, I do. In fact, I usually sleep longer than that!
Faisal: Well, maybe instead of watching TV, you could get more exercise.
Alex: Like what?
Faisal: You could work out at the gym.
Alex: But I don't have time. I'm too busy.
Faisal: Really? How do you get to work in the morning?
Alex: I drive my car, of course.
Faisal: Why?! It's only a mile to your office. You should ride a bike or walk.

G Practice the conversation in pairs. Switch roles and practice it again.

✓ **GOAL CHECK** Give Advice about Healthy Habits

In pairs, ask *Do you...?* questions about the activities in **B**. Give each other advice.

> Do you get eight hours of sleep every night?

> No, I don't.

> You should get more sleep.

GOAL Compare Lifestyles

Listening

Ben

Beata

Kim

A 🎧 53 Look at the photos. Guess who is healthy or unhealthy. Rank the people's lifestyles from healthy to unhealthy. Compare your answers in small groups. Then listen and check.

Healthy lifestyle ————————————————— Unhealthy lifestyle

B 🎧 53 Listen again and complete the table.

	Ben	Beata	Kim
Exercise	Sometimes he goes to the gym on Sundays.		She works in her garden.
Food and diet		She eats a big breakfast of healthy foods.	
Unhealthy habit	Smoking		

PRONUNCIATION: *Have to*

When talking about obligation, people often reduce and connect the words *have to*.
Have to sounds like *hafta* when this happens: /hæv tu/ ➜ /hæftə/.

C 🎧 54 Listen to each sentence two times. Notice the pronunciation of *have to* and repeat the sentences.

I have to meet clients.
I often have to grab a hamburger.
I have to stop smoking.

D 🎧 55 Listen to the sentences and check (✓) *Full Form* or *Reduced Form*.

	Full Form	Reduced Form
1. I have to drink less coffee.		
2. They have to go to the gym.		
3. We have to eat more healthy food.		
4. You have to lose weight.		
5. Meg and Yuki have to work late.		

In pairs, take turns saying the sentences in **D** with the full or reduced form of *have to*. Your partner will say if you are using the full or reduced form.

Conversation

F Answer the questions for yourself. Then survey two classmates.

Lifestyle Choices	Me		Classmate 1 Name _____		Classmate 2 Name _____	
Do you play computer games?	Yes → No	____ hours a day	Yes → No	____ hours a day	Yes → No	____ hours a day
Do you eat fresh vegetables?	Yes → No	____ a day	Yes → No	____ a day	Yes → No	____ a day
Do you spend time on social media?	Yes → No	____ hours a day	Yes → No	____ hours a day	Yes → No	____ hours a day
Do you work out most days?	Yes → No	____ hours a day	Yes → No	____ hours a day	Yes → No	____ hours a day
Do you drink coffee or tea every day?	Yes → No	____ cups a day	Yes → No	____ cups a day	Yes → No	____ cups a day
Do you eat sugary foods and drinks?	Yes → No	____ a day	Yes → No	____ a day	Yes → No	____ a day

Do you play computer games?

Yes, I do.

How many hours a day do you play?

Two hours!

✓ GOAL CHECK Compare Lifestyles

Work with a new partner. Take turns presenting the results of the survey. For each question, compare yourself and the classmates you surveyed. Say who has the healthiest lifestyle.

Salma works out in the gym every day for two hours and doesn't eat sugary foods or drinks.

Yahir eats about five servings of sugary foods and drinks per day and never works out. Salma has a healthier lifestyle.

C GOAL Ask about Happiness

Language Expansion: Compound Adjectives

A Read the news report. Which country is the happiest in the world?

The World Happiness Report uses information from 156 countries to decide which country is the happiest in the world. People in these countries are the most stress-free and the least overworked. In 2018, Finland was number one.

a. works too much

b. ~~delicious~~

c. without worries or problems

d. not high in calories

e. makes you happy

f. produced in your own garden

g. all your life

h. not made in a factory

B Look at the compound adjectives above in blue. Compound adjectives have two words joined together. What are the two words in each compound adjective?

C Match the compound adjectives to their meanings in the box.

1. mouthwatering ____b____
2. homemade _____
3. heartwarming _____
4. lifelong _____

5. stress-free _____
6. homegrown _____
7. overworked _____
8. low-calorie _____

D Complete the sentences. Use adjectives from **C**.

1. Kevin and I went to kindergarten together. We are _____ friends.
2. When I was a child, my father had a vegetable garden. We ate lots of _____ fruit and vegetables.
3. I have to work long hours, and I'm always tired. I think I am _____.
4. My grandmother makes the best _____ chicken soup in the world! It's absolutely _____.

The city of Porvoo, Finland. How do you think a place like this is stress-free?

E **MY WORLD** Choose three compound adjectives in **C** and write sentences with the adjectives about your lifestyle.

Grammar

Questions with *How*	
How much exercise do you get?	**How much:** quantity of non-count nouns
How many cigarettes do you smoke a day?	**How many:** quantity of count nouns
How old is your father?	**How old:** age
How long did your grandfather live?	**How long:** length or a period of time
How often do you go to the gym?	**How often:** frequency

F Write the missing words. Then match the questions to the answers.

1. How ___often___ does Mike go swimming? _____   **a.** She's about 85.
2. How _____ is Akuru's grandmother? _____   **b.** Until I'm 80.
3. How _____ junk food do you eat? _____   **c.** 3 or 4 servings a day.
4. How _____ do you think you will live? _____   **d.** Not much.
5. How _____ vegetables does he eat? _____   **e.** Once a week.

G Make questions with *How* for these answers. In pairs, ask and answer the questions.

Once a week.   27 years old.   About 2 hours.   Not much.

Conversation

H 🎧 56 Listen to the conversation. What are questions 1 and 2 in the happiness survey? How happy is Mr. Lopez? Then practice the conversation in pairs.

Interviewer:	Hello, I'm asking questions for a survey. We're studying people's happiness. Can I ask you a few questions?
Mr. Lopez:	Sure, go ahead.
Interviewer:	OK, question one. How many hours do you work a week?
Mr. Lopez:	I think I work around 80 hours a week.
Interviewer:	80 hours! That's a lot!
Mr. Lopez:	I know. I'm really overworked.
Interviewer:	Question 2 is about exercise. How much exercise do you get a week?
Mr. Lopez:	Not much because of my job. I go to the gym about once a month.

SPEAKING STRATEGY

Approximation
When you don't know the exact answer, use *approximation* language.
About once a month.
Around 80 hours a week.
Almost twenty cigarettes a day.

✓ GOAL CHECK Ask about Happiness

1. Write three more questions for the happiness survey in **H**.
2. Interview classmates with your questions and the ones in the conversation.
3. In small groups, discuss your results. How happy is your class?

D GOAL Discuss the Importance of Sleep

Reading

A Do you often look at a screen (e.g., a phone or laptop) before you go to sleep? Do you think it's bad for your health? Why?

B Read the article. Match the title to each paragraph.

　a. A twenty-first century problem

　b. The problem of light and screens

　c. Why do we need to sleep?

C Read again. Answer each question. Circle *Yes*, *No*, or *Doesn't say.*

　1. Is sleep good for our health?　　　(Yes)　No　Doesn't say

　2. Do we study and work better　　　Yes　No　Doesn't say
　　　with eight hours of sleep?

　3. Does regular sleep help　　　　Yes　No　Doesn't say
　　　students' grades in school?

　4. Do Americans sleep less than　　Yes　No　Doesn't say
　　　people of other nationalities?

　5. Does the movement of the sun　　Yes　No　Doesn't say
　　　affect our natural clock?

　6. Does blue light affect our sleep?　Yes　No　Doesn't say

　7. Should we check our phones　　　Yes　No　Doesn't say
　　　before we sleep?

　8. Does the writer think we will take　Yes　No　Doesn't say
　　　the advice of medical experts?

D Complete this summary using words from the article.

Sleep is good for physical and (1) _mental_ health. It helps stop
(2)_____ and keeps us healthy. We also study and work
(3)_____ when we sleep for (4)_____ hours. But in the
twenty-first century, we aren't getting enough sleep. One reason
is that we stay up (5)_____ or (6)_____ all night. Another
reason is that (7)_____ light from screens keeps us awake.
As a result, medical experts advise us to stop looking at screens
(8)_____ hour before bed.

✓ GOAL CHECK

In groups, prepare a presentation called "Why sleep is good for you."

　1. List all the reasons why sleep is good for you. Use ideas
　　　from the article and add two of your own ideas.

　2. Join another group and take turns giving your presentation.
　　　Did you give similar reasons? What was different?

This man is sleeping on a subway platform in Japan. The Japanese term *inemuri* means "sleeping while present." As people work more and get less sleep at night, this is more common.

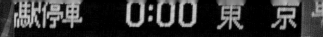

The Need for Sleep

_____ For thousands of years, humans have asked the question: "Why do we sleep?" and modern scientists are still trying to find the answer. But one thing we do know is that it's good for our physical and mental health. Physically, sleep helps prevent sickness and keeps our body healthy. Mentally, we study and work better when we sleep for about eight hours the previous night. Sleep might also stop **dementia** when you are older.

_____ In this century, **lack** of sleep is becoming a big problem. The average American sleeps less than seven hours a night—that's two hours less than a century ago. Our modern 24-hour-day lifestyle means that more and more of us are working at different times of the day—and night. We often **stay up** late into the night, and some of us even work all night and sleep during the day. This is a problem because our body's natural clock is connected with the movement of the sun. In other words, if we don't sleep at night for long periods, it can be bad for our health.

_____ But perhaps the biggest problem for sleep comes from electric lights and screens. Modern cities use bright LED lights through the night, which changes the way we sleep. In addition, the screens of our computers, tablets, and smartphones all send out blue light. The bluer and brighter the light, the more difficult it is to get tired and go to sleep. As a result, some medical experts now suggest that we shouldn't watch more than two hours of television per day, and that we should stop looking at screens (including phones) one hour before we go to bed. But since light and screens are so important in our lives, how many of us will take this advice?

dementia a medical problem with the brain that changes memory and personality (usually in older people)
lack not enough (of something)
stay up not go to bed

Communication

A 🎧 58 Listen to three pieces of music. Check (✓) the adjectives to describe your feelings about the music and write your own words.

	Happy	Relaxed	Stressed	Excited	Bored	Positive	Your words
1.							
2.							
3.							

Dancing

Drawing or painting

Gardening

Jogging

Listening to music

Playing video games

Singing / karaoke

Walking in a park

Watching TV

B Read about Valorie Salimpoor and answer the questions.

Valorie Salimpoor is a neuroscientist. One day, Valorie was in her car and felt unhappy. Then, suddenly there was some classical music on the radio. Immediately, she felt much better and she wanted to understand why. Valorie started to study what happens to the brain when people listen to different types of music. With her evidence, she thinks music can be good for our mental health because "it's really an exercise for your whole brain."

1. How did she feel one day? What happened?

2. From her research, what does she think about music?

C **MY WORLD** Do you agree with Valorie's ideas about music? What types of music make you feel better?

D In pairs, discuss which of the activities in the box to the left are good for your mental health. Give reasons. Do you think any of these activities are bad for your mental health? Compare your ideas in small groups.

Studies show that dance is good for your mental and physical health.

Writing

E Read the paragraph about a student's hobbies and answer the questions.

> I love dancing and, in my opinion, it's good for your physical and mental health. First, dancing keeps you in shape because you are always moving around. In addition, it's social because you meet new people and have fun. Also, when you learn new dances, you have to memorize them and use your brain. In conclusion, I think everyone should go dancing to get healthy.

1. What is her hobby?

2. Why is it good for her physical health?

3. Why is it good for her mental health?

F Read the information about paragraph structure. Then find the topic sentence, supporting sentences, and concluding sentence in the paragraph in **E**.

WRITING SKILL: Paragraph Structure

Topic sentence	→	The first sentence is the main subject of your paragraph. Useful phrases: *I like ... because ..., I think ..., In my opinion, ...*
Supporting sentences	→	Add two or three sentences to give more information and reasons for your opinion. They should support your topic. Useful phrases: *Firstly, / First, / First of all, Secondly, / Second, Also, In addition,*
Concluding sentence	→	Not all paragraphs have this sentence, but sometimes it's useful because it summarizes the main ideas. Useful phrases: *To conclude, In conclusion, / To sum up, I think ...*

G Make a new paragraph. Put these sentences in the correct order from 1 to 5.

_____ In addition, when you grow your own vegetables, you also eat healthy food.

_____ Third, I spend time outside with nature, so it's stress-free and very relaxing.

_____ In my free time, I like gardening because it's good for my physical and mental health.

_____ First, you have to move around a lot, so it's good exercise.

_____ To sum up, I think gardening is great for my body and my brain.

 GOAL CHECK Explain Healthy Activities

1. Plan a paragraph about a healthy hobby or activity. Make notes and list the different reasons why it is good for your health.

2. Write your paragraph using your notes.

3. Exchange your paragraph with a partner. Does your partner's paragraph have:

- a topic sentence?
- supporting sentences?
- a concluding sentence?

VIDEO JOURNAL

LIVING PAST 100

A Look at the photo of Bama County. Circle the adjectives that you think describe this region.

crowded   exciting   healthy   interesting
noisy   polluted   quiet   stress-free

B Do you think Bama County is a good place for a vacation? Why?

C In the video about Bama County, you will see four different types of people. Complete the sentences with the correct person.

centenarian   health tourist   researcher   villager

1. A _____ studies a subject and looks for evidence and information.

2. A _____ lives in the countryside without a lot of other people.

3. A _____ lives to be 100 years old.

4. A _____ goes on vacation to improve their physical and mental health.

D Watch the video. Circle **T** for *true* or **F** for *false*.

1. Bama County is in China.   **T**   **F**

2. It's famous because all the villagers are centenarians.   **T**   **F**

3. Every day, Huang Zhongkang goes swimming.   **T**   **F**

4. Four years ago, Yao Xuchu had a stroke.   **T**   **F**

5. Sometimes tourists leave garbage.   **T**   **F**

6. The village is going to build a new eco-resort.   **T**   **F**

E Discuss the questions in pairs.

1. Do you want to live to be 100 years old?

2. What do you think you should do to live to be 100?

3. Do you know anyone who is 100 years old? What is their lifestyle?

F Watch the video again and make notes about the questions in the table.

What are some reasons for long life in Bama County?	
Why do tourists come to the county? What do they do?	
What are the advantages of tourism for the region?	

G In groups, imagine that a company wants to build a new resort for tourists near you. Brainstorm the advantages and disadvantages of more tourists. Use the chart and your notebook.

Advantages	Disadvantages
income for local people	*more garbage*

H Join another group and compare your lists. Then discuss the questions:

1. Are there more advantages or disadvantages?

2. Should you let the company build the resort?

Cliffs and a river in Bama County, Guangxi, China

These students are graduating from Whittier College in California, US.

Look at the photo and answer the questions.

1 What is their achievement?

2 What personal achievements are you proud of?

UNIT 11 GOALS

A. Talk about Responsibilities

B. Interview for a Job

C. Talk about Personal Achievements

D. Plan for Success

E. Write a Resume

GOAL Talk about Responsibilities

Vocabulary

A Label the photos with the chores from the box.

buy the groceries	clean your room	clean the car	cook dinner
take out the trash	vacuum the floor	walk the dog	wash the dishes

WORD FOCUS

Clean is used for different chores around the house: *clean your room / the car / the floor*

1. _____ 2. _____ 3. _____

4. _____ 5. _____ 6. _____

7. _____ 8. _____

B Categorize the chores in **A** next to the comments below. You can use the same chore more than once.

1. "These chores are easy." _____

2. "These chores are boring." _____

3. "I often do these chores." _____

4. "I never do these chores." _____

C In pairs, compare your answers in **B**. For the chores in item 4, say who does those chores in your house.

> I often wash the dishes. I never cook dinner. My parents do.

Grammar

Present Perfect	
Statement	I **have finished** my homework. / He **has finished** his homework.
Negative	I **haven't finished**. / She **hasn't finished**.
Yes / No Questions	**Have** you **finished** your homework? / **Has** he **finished**?
Short Answers	Yes, I **have**. / Yes, he **has**. No, I **haven't**. / No, she **hasn't**.
Wh- Questions	**What have** you **done** today?
Form the present perfect with *has / have* + past participle. We can use the present perfect (like the simple past) to talk about completed actions in the past, but without saying when they happened.	
Past Participles	
Regular verbs end in *-ed*: *walk* → *has / have walked*, *clean* → *has / have cleaned* Irregular verbs have irregular past participles: *cut* → *has / have cut*, *buy* → *has / have bought*	

D 🎧 59 Listen to a conversation between a mother and daughter. Check (✓) the things they have done. Put an ✗ for the things they haven't done.

1. ✓ walk the dog   3. ☐ finish homework   5. ☐ cook dinner

2. ☐ vacuum the floor   4. ☐ buy some groceries

E 🎧 59 Complete the conversation with the present perfect. Then listen and check your answers.

Mom: Hi, Lyn. I'm home.

Lyn: Hi, Mom.

Mom: (1) _____ you _____ (walk) the dog?

Lyn: Yes, I (2) _____. And I (3) _____ (vacuum) the floor.

Mom: Wonderful! (4) _____ you _____ (finish) your homework?

Lyn: No, I (5) _____. I'm going to do it now.

Mom: OK. Are you hungry? I bought some groceries, so I'm going to cook dinner.

Lyn: Great!

F Practice the conversation in pairs. Switch roles and practice it again.

> Have you walked the dog?

> Yes, I have.

G Look at the chores in **A**. Pick four chores and put a check (✓) next to them. In pairs, take turns asking and answering questions about the chores. Say you've done the ones with checks.

 GOAL CHECK Talk about Responsibilities

1. Make a list of chores or activities you have done this week.

2. In pairs, talk about the chores and activities you have done this week.

> What have you done this week?

> I've finished all my homework.

GOAL Interview for a Job

Listening

A Read the job ad. What is the job? What skills do you need for the job?

B 🎧 60 Read the questions. Then listen to two interviews and check (✓) the questions you hear. You will hear two questions in both interviews. One question is not asked in either.

	1	2
1. Have you graduated from college?		
2. Have you ever traveled abroad?		
3. What is the most interesting place you've visited?		
4. Have you worked with customers?		
5. Have you worked as a tour guide?		
6. Who is the most interesting person you have met?		
7. Have you taken any English language exams?		
8. Have you ever managed a group of people?		
9. Have you passed your driving test?		

C 🎧 60 Listen again and write notes in the table about each topic.

	Ms. Harmon	**Mr. Liu**
Subjects in college		
Travel and places visited		
Experience as a tour guide		
Driver's license		
Experience with groups		

Bromo Tengger Semeru National Park, on the island of Java, is one of the most famous landmarks in Indonesia.

D Who should get the job? Discuss in pairs.

E 🎧 **61** Listen to the examples. Notice the pronunciation of the reduced forms.

PRONUNCIATION: Reduced Forms of *have*

Full Form	Reduced Form
I have	I've – /aɪv/
have you	/hæv jə/
you have	you've – /juv/
has he	/hæz i/
she has	she's – /ʃiz/

F 🎧 **62** Listen to the sentences. Check (✓) the correct column.

	Full Form	Reduced Form
1. I have studied English and history.		
2. She has worked as a tour guide.		
3. He has managed people.		
4. She has passed her driving test.		
5. Has he coached a team?		
6. Have you ever traveled abroad?		

G In pairs, take turns saying a sentence in **F** with the full form or reduced form of the *has / have*. Can your partner say which form you used?

SPEAKING STRATEGY

Job Interviews
Thank you for coming to the interview.
Let's begin.
Now, a practical question: Have you...?
Great. / That's interesting.
One last question...
We'll contact you next Tuesday.

GOAL CHECK Interview for a Job

You are going to role play two interviews using the ads below. In the first interview, Student A is the interviewer and Student B is the interviewee. Change roles for the second interview. Before each interview, pick an ad together and prepare a list of ten questions for your partner. You can use some of the questions in **B**, as well as your own.

═══ WANTED ═══

Summer School Assistant

A summer school is looking for a person to help the manager. The children are between 7 and 13 years old. Experience with children is necessary. An interest in playing team sports and games is an advantage.

Clothing Store Associate

A clothing store needs an associate to help with customers. We are looking for a friendly person with good communication skills. Experience working at a store is not necessary (training is provided). An interest in clothes and fashion is an advantage.

Have you worked with children?

Yes, I have. I coached a baseball team.

C GOAL Talk about Personal Achievements

Language Expansion: Personal Achievements

A Read about Ciril Jazbec. What has he achieved?

Ciril Jazbec is a photographer from Slovenia. As a child, he wanted to be a National Geographic photographer, and he became one in 2014. A couple of years ago, he went to Greenland and took this photo for a story in *National Geographic Magazine*. He has worked around the world and he's won awards for photos of people in places like Bhutan, Kenya, and Alaska.

get a promotion

graduate from
   high school /
   college

learn a language

pass your driving
   test

run a marathon

travel abroad

B Label the pictures with the achievements from the box.

1. _____

2. _____

3. _____

4. _____

5. _____

6. _____

C In groups, discuss the achievements in **B**. Rank them from 1 to 6 and give reasons. (1 = most difficult to achieve, 6 = easiest to achieve.)

Grammar

D Compare the sentences (a and b) about the past. Then answer the questions.

   a. He has worked around the world.

   b. As a child, he wanted to be a National Geographic photographer.

   1. Which sentence doesn't say when the action happened?

   2. Which sentence describes an action at a specific time?

   3. What verb tense is used in each sentence?

Present Perfect vs. Simple Past	
Present Perfect	Simple Past
We often ask present perfect questions to ask about life experiences. **Have you ever been** to another country? For negative answers, you can use *never*. **No, I've never been** to another country.	Use time expressions like *yesterday, last week,* and *in 2010* with the simple past. They **went** to France **last year**. **Did you go** to work **yesterday**?

E Underline the present perfect verbs and circle the simple past verbs in **A**.

F Underline the correct words to complete the conversations.

A: *Have you ever | Did you ever* been to Europe?

B: No, I *haven't | didn't*, but I've been to Asia.

A: When did you go there?

B: I *'ve gone | went* there two years ago.

A: *Did you study | Have you studied* any languages there?

B: Yes, two. Korean and Chinese.

A: Wow! I *'ve never studied | never studied* Chinese. Was it hard to learn?

B: Yes, it was, but I *'ve lived | lived* in Beijing for a year, so that helped.

Conversation

G 🎧 63 Listen to the conversation. Who started his own business?

Alfredo: Hi, Pete. I haven't seen you for a long time. What's new?

Pete: Lots! I quit my job and I've started <u>my own computer business</u>.

Alfredo: Congratulations! When did you <u>open the business</u>?

Pete: Eight months ago. It's going really well. What about you?

Alfredo: I'm still working at the bank, but I've <u>gone back to school.</u>

Pete: Great, when did you do that?

Alfredo: Last month.

H Practice the conversation in pairs. Switch roles and practice it again.

I Change the underlined words and practice the conversation again.

SPEAKING STRATEGY

We often ask questions about recent activities using the present perfect, then ask for more information using the simple past.
A: What have you been doing lately?
B: I've started my own business.
A: Oh! When did you open it?

✓ GOAL CHECK Talk about Personal Achievements

1. Prepare five *Have you ever...?* questions about your partner's achievements. You can use achievements from **B** or your own ideas.

2. Interview your partner. If they answer "Yes," ask for more information.

Have you ever run a marathon?   Yes, I have.   When did you run it?

D GOAL Plan for Success

Reading

A In groups, try to answer the questions about "famous firsts." Do you know any other famous firsts in history or in your country?

1. Who was the first astronaut in space?

   a. Yuri Gagarin   **b.** Sally Ride   **c.** Neil Armstrong

2. Who was the first female musician to sell more than 300 million records?

   a. Beyoncé   **b.** Madonna   **c.** Taylor Swift

3. Who was the first person to run a mile in 4 minutes?

   a. Usain Bolt   **b.** Michael Johnson   **c.** Roger Bannister

B Look at the photo and the title of the article. Write five words you expect to read in the article. Compare in pairs.

C Read the article and answer the questions.

1. Check your words in **B**. Are they in the article?

2. Was Eliud successful?

D Read the ways to plan for success as a marathon runner. Which six are in the article about Eliud?

1. Prepare for about two years. ☐

2. Work with a team of experts. ☐

3. Get up early every morning. ☐

4. Use technology to study your running. ☐

5. Plan the food you eat. ☐

6. Ask other people for information and advice. ☐

7. Take regular breaks. ☐

8. Run with other athletes. ☐

E Words 1–4 are from the article. Match each to a similar word.

1. train _____   **a.** timetable

2. schedule _____   **b.** achieve

3. system _____   **c.** plan

4. manage to do _____ **d.** practice

✓ GOAL CHECK

1. Write five sentences about how you plan for success in learning English. Use the ideas and words in **D** and **E**.

2. Share your ideas in groups. Work as a team and learn new ideas from each other.

BEING THE FIRST IN LESS THAN TWO HOURS

Eliud Kipchoge is a marathon runner from Kenya. He's won eleven gold medals so far and many people think he's the most successful marathon runner in the world. He holds the world record for the fastest marathon. No one has ever run a marathon faster than Eliud.

But for Eliud that is not enough because, in 2017, he tried to become the first human to run a marathon in less than two hours. It took two years to prepare for the run, and during this time, Eliud worked with a team of experts. They used technology to study everything about his running: his training schedule, his breathing, his diet, his running shoes, and his movements.

For Eliud, this teamwork was very important. He said, "I get information from scientists, information from the management, and from the coaching system." As well as taking ideas and advice from his team, Eliud also trained for the run with other athletes. "You cannot train alone and expect to run a fast time."

After two years of planning and training, the big day arrived and Eliud ran the distance of 26.2 miles on a track in Milan, Italy. His time was good for most of the race and he finished it in a record time of 2 hours, 25 seconds; but it wasn't fast enough. Eliud described the final part of the run: "I felt a little bit tired in my legs and I tried to **pick it up**, but it was too late."

So, if Eliud can't run a marathon in under 2 hours, is it possible for any human? Maybe in the future, as technology gets better, someone might achieve a time of 1 hour 59 minutes and 59 seconds. Eliud says, "The goal was to **break the** two-hour **barrier** and I didn't manage to do that. But the world record is now just 25 seconds away. I think it will be easy for another human being."

pick it up go faster
break the barrier manage to beat a record

Eliud Kipchoge runs in a race in Kavarna, Bulgaria.

E GOAL Write a Resume

Communication

A Have you ever written a resume for a job or completed an application form for school? What information did you include?

B In groups, look at the advice for writing a resume. Discuss if each statement is true or false in your country and give reasons.

1. Write about every school you have been to.		T	F
2. List all your work experience (starting with the most recent job).		T	F
3. Include a photo.		T	F
4. Add information about your hobbies.		T	F
5. Always write in full sentences.		T	F
6. Give two references for people who know you well.		T	F
7. Use a simple and clear computer font.		T	F
8. Use lots of different colors.		T	F

C In pairs, discuss Linh's resume. Does she follow your advice in **B**? What information is missing?

Linh H. Brenner

Personal details

Nationality: Vietnamese and American
Address: Apartment 5, 109 Parkway Avenue,
San Francisco, CA, USA
Email: l_brenner@brenner.vn
Date of birth: 27 July, 1999

Education

2018–Present	MA in Business Administration, Golden Gate University
2015–2018	BA in English and Economics, University of Da Nang

Work experience

August, 2018–Present	Part-time server in the university student cafe.
June–August, 2018	School assistant in the summer with children ages 6 to 9.

Skills

Languages: Vietnamese, English, French
Computers: Word, Powerpoint, and iMovie
California driver's license

Interests

Member of the college soccer team and sailing club. Taking photos of nature and making videos.

Reference

Dr. Susan McFadden, Faculty of Business, Golden Gate University

---

Writing

D People often spell these words incorrectly on resumes. Find these words in the resume in **C** and check (✓) the correct spelling.

1. personal ☐   personnal ☐   5. buisness ☐   business ☐
2. detales ☐   details ☐   6. childen ☐   children ☐
3. address ☐   adress ☐   7. license ☐   lisense ☐
4. experience ☐ experiance ☐   8. intrests ☐   interests ☐

E Read the resume again and check (✓) the types of words that need a capital letter.

1. First name, middle initial, and last name ☐
2. The first letter of sentence ☐
3. Nationality and country ☐
4. Cities and streets ☐
5. Months ☐
6. Seasons ☐
7. Qualifications and courses ☐
8. Languages ☐
9. Names of sports and hobbies ☐
10. Titles of people ☐

F Circle five spelling mistakes and underline five mistakes with capital letters in this description.

My name's Robert dawson and I'm australian. I have a degree in Buisness Studys from sydney Univercity, and I have experiance working for a computer company. my intrests are Soccer and going to the movies.

 GOAL CHECK Write a Resume

1. Write your resume.
2. Exchange your resumes in pairs and check for mistakes.

People working in the cafe at the Google headquarters in Dublin, Ireland

VIDEO JOURNAL

WASFIA'S JOURNEY

A Read the article.

1. Who is Wasfia? Where is she from?
2. What has she achieved? When did she achieve it?

> **Wasfia becomes the first Bangladeshi to climb the seven highest mountains**
>
> *November 26, 2015*
>
> At 10:19 am on November 18, Wasfia Nazreen reached the summit of Carstensz Pyramid, the highest mountain in Oceania / Australasia. After the climb she said, "Carstensz Pyramid was the toughest and remotest mountain I have ever climbed in my life."
>
> Wasfia has now achieved her final goal—to become the first Bangladeshi to climb the highest mountains on seven continents: Carstensz, as well as Mount Elbrus in Europe, Mount Aconcagua in South America, Denali in North America, Mount Vinson Massif in Antarctica, Mount Kilimanjaro in Africa, and Mount Everest in Asia.

B Watch the video and number the events in the order that you see them.

___1___ Wasfia is climbing up Mount Kilimanjaro.

_____ She's playing with two girls.

_____ She's holding the flag of Bangladesh at the top of a mountain.

_____ She's meditating in a temple.

_____ She's walking up steps.

_____ She's inside a tent.

_____ She's looking at photos of women from Bangladesh.

_____ She's talking to a class of girls.

_____ She's flying in a helicopter.

_____ She's in an airport.

C Watch again and choose the correct answer.

1. In the past, when she said she's from Bangladesh, what did people say?
   a. "I don't know where that is."
   b. "You get floods."
   c. a and b

2. When she decided to climb the seven mountains, who believed she could do it?
   a. No one
   b. Someone
   c. Everyone

3. What is the third part of her training?
   a. Cardio training
   b. High altitude training
   c. Meditation

4. Her climbing teacher was Ngima Grimen. How did he die?
   a. In a climbing accident
   b. In a motorbike accident
   c. In a car accident

5. What does the first girl want to be when she grows up?
   a. A teacher
   b. A climber
   c. A doctor

D Discuss these questions in pairs. Then tell the class your opinions.

1. How do you think Wasfia felt about people's ideas about Bangladesh?
2. Why do you think no one believed Wasfia could climb the seven mountains?
3. How can Wasfia's achievement change people's opinion of her and of other women?

E In groups, think of a person who has achieved something important. (The person could be famous or someone you know.) Plan a video documentary about this person. Answer the questions to the right. Then share your ideas with the class.

- Who is the person?
- What is their achievement?
- Who will you interview in the documentary?
- Where will you film the documentary?
- Will you have narration? What will you say?

WORD FOCUS

altitude height above sea level
cardio heart exercise
flood too much water after it rains
summit the top of a mountain

155

A cyclist comes to a fork in the road in the Altiplano in Bolivia.

UNIT 12 GOALS

A. Give Advice about Money

B. Choose What to Use

C. Make Decisions about Money

D. Plan How to Raise Money

E. Compare and Contrast Options

157

GOAL Give Advice about Money

Vocabulary

A Read the article from a student magazine. What advice does the article give? Do you think it's good advice?

STUDENT LIFE
Managing your Money

Congratulations! You just received your first student loan. So now it's decision time. How are you going to spend it? On a new phone? Or some cool sneakers? Well, don't! Before you spend a penny of it, make a budget. Compare the amount of your loan with your expenses (rent, transportation, food).

If you don't have enough money for the year, maybe you can borrow more. But if you borrow money from a bank, you pay interest, so—if possible—ask a friend or family member to lend you the money. Or, a lot of students have part-time jobs to earn some money. And if you are a student, you don't pay much in taxes. With the income from the job, try to save some of your extra money for later in the year.

WORD FOCUS

lend to ≠ borrow from
Use these verbs to talk about loans:
*The bank **lends** money **to** you.* = the bank gives you money
*You **borrow** money **from** the bank.* = you receive money from the bank

B Write the words in blue next to the definitions.

1. money that students borrow to help pay for college: _student loan_
2. money you receive from work: _____
3. money you spend: _____
4. receive money that you have to return in the future: _____
5. give someone money that they have to return in the future: _____
6. a spending plan: _____
7. put money in the bank for the future: _____
8. the percentage (%) you pay when you borrow money: _____
9. money you give to the government: _____
10. get money from working: _____

C **MY WORLD** In pairs, follow the steps below.

1. Make a list of all your monthly expenses (e.g., bus pass, clothes, food, etc.). Write them in the table.
2. Compare your answers with another pair.

Need	Optional

Grammar

Real Conditionals: The Zero Conditional	
If Clause (Simple Present)	Main Clause (Simple Present or Imperative)
If you **borrow** money from a bank,	you **pay** interest.
If you **receive** a student loan,	**don't spend** it all on new clothes!
We use the zero conditional to: • talk about facts or things that are usually true. • give instructions or advice.	

D Match the clauses. Does each main clause talk about facts or give instructions?

1. If you get a job, _____

2. If you use a credit card, _____

3. If you bring your lunch, _____

4. If you borrow money from friends, _____

5. If you put your card in an ATM, _____

a. you pay interest.

b. remember to pay them back!

c. you earn money.

d. it's much cheaper.

e. you get money.

E In pairs, complete the sentences in your own words. Use the simple present or an imperative form. Then compare your sentences with another pair.

1. If you save 20% of your income every month, _____.

2. If you spend more money than you earn, _____.

3. If you borrow money from your parents, _____.

Conversation

F 🎧 65 Listen to the conversation. What does the tourist want? What instructions and advice does Jim give?

Tourist: Excuse me. Can you help me?

Jim: Sure, what's the problem?

Tourist: I'm from Japan and I don't have any dollars. I only have Japanese yen.

Jim: If you want to change money, go to the currency exchange.

Tourist: Where is it?

Jim: If you go down this street, there's a currency exchange on the right.

Tourist: Oh, thank you very much.

G Practice the conversation in pairs. Switch roles and practice it again.

H Make new conversations between the tourist and Jim. The tourist wants to:

• get money from an ATM.   • find a bank.   • buy souvenirs.

 GOAL CHECK Give Advice about Money

1. Write down three things you want to do with money.

2. In pairs, take turns saying what you want to do and giving advice.

> If you want to buy a car, borrow the money from your parents.

B GOAL Choose What to Use

Luzinterruptus is an art collective from Madrid, Spain. They take the plastic trash of a city and put it in the city's most beautiful places to show the impact it has. This photo is from central Madrid.

Listening

A Look at the photo. Is this a problem in your country? How can we solve the problem?

B You are going to listen to a podcast about Marie McGory. She packed these items for a trip to Belize. Match the words to the pictures.

a. a bamboo spoon and fork

b. food containers

c. a glass straw

d. a reuseable bag

e. reuseable water bottles

C 🎧 66 Listen and circle **T** for *true* or **F** for *false*.

1. Humans produce about 450 million tons of plastic a year.   T   F
2. A lot of plastic is in oceans and on beaches.   T   F
3. Everyone is trying to stop using single-use plastic.   T   F
4. Marie tried to travel without using single-use plastic.   T   F
5. She took two water bottles because she might lose one of them.   T   F
6. She took containers so she didn't have to buy fast food in plastic.   T   F
7. You need to tell the waiter that you don't want a plastic straw.   T   F
8. Not using single-use plastic is expensive.   T   F

D 🎧 67 Listen and write the missing verbs in these zero conditional sentences.

1. If we _____ using single-use plastic, we _____ the problem.

2. If you _____ two water bottles, it _____ enough water for a long trip.

3. If you _____ food containers, you can _____ snacks in them.

4. If you _____ to a cafe and _____ a drink, _____ the waiter that you don't need a plastic straw.

PRONUNCIATION: Conditional Intonation

In conditional sentences, the intonation usually rises toward the end of the *if* clause and falls toward the end of the main clause.

E 🎧 67 Listen to the sentences in **D** again. Draw arrows to show rise and fall.

If we stop using single-use plastic, we solve the problem.

✓ **GOAL CHECK** Choose What to Use

1. In groups, think about the last 24 hours. Fill in the first column of the chart. Write the plastic items you used.

2. Which items were single-use plastic? Which were reuseable? Check (✓) the correct column.

3. If you used single-use plastic items, which can you avoid using? How?

4. Join another group and tell them about your choices.

Plastic Item	Single-Use?	Reusable?

If I need a bag, I don't need a plastic one. I can use a paper bag.

If I pack a lunch, I can use a reusable food container.

C GOAL Make Decisions about Money

Language Expansion: Money Verbs

A Which countries use these currencies? Some have more than one answer.

> Dollar   Euro   Peso   Pound   Yuan

B Read the article. Underline five verbs we use with the word *money.*

Money Travel Tips

If you travel abroad, you'll need different currencies. There are yen in Japan, dong in Vietnam, sols in Peru, reals in Brazil, and dollars in many countries. It can be confusing! Here are some tips:

- Plan how much money you will spend each day. Then, calculate the amount in the local currency.
- If you change your money before you leave, it'll be cheaper than at airports or hotels.
- When you arrive, carry your money in different places: in your wallet, your bag, and your pocket. Then, if someone steals any, you won't lose all of it.

C In pairs, write the money verbs from the box in the correct column. Then compare your answers with another pair. Do you agree?

borrow	carry
change	earn
find	lend
lose	make
save	spend
steal	win

Positive	Neutral	Negative
save		

D Choose five money verbs and write a sentence with each one. Then read your sentences in pairs, but don't say the verb. Can your partner guess the missing verb?

> My grandmother plays the lottery every week, but she never ... any money.

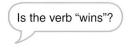 Is the verb "wins"?

Grammar

Real Conditionals: The First Conditional	
If Clause (Simple Present)	Main Clause (*Will* for Future)
If you **take** a trip to the US,	you **will need** dollars.
If you **change** your money before you leave,	it **will be** cheaper.
Use the first conditional to talk about a future possible action (*if* clause) and the result (main clause).	

Put the words in the correct order to make a first conditional sentence.

1. a bigger car / some money / we borrow / If / we will be able to buy
   <u>If we borrow some money, we will be able to buy a bigger car.</u>

2. a new job / more money / I will have / I get / If
   _____

3. on vacation / we spend too much / If / to go / we won't be able
   _____

4. you won't have to / I / use your credit card / If / lend you $100
   _____

Conversation

F 🎧 68 Listen to the conversation and underline the first conditional sentences. Then practice the conversation with a partner.

Gaby: OK. What's the best way to travel from Los Angeles to San Diego?
Sharon: Well, if we take the bus, it'll be cheaper.
Gaby: But sometimes I get sick on buses. What if we go by train?
Sharon: It's quicker, but only by one hour.
Gaby: Or we could fly.
Sharon: But if we take the plane, we won't have any money left!

SPEAKING STRATEGY
Talking about Choices
If we take ..., it'll be ...
What if we ...?
Will it be ...?
If we ..., we won't ...
Or we could ...

✔ **GOAL CHECK** Make Decisions about Money

1. In pairs, plan a six-day trip to California. You each have $300 to spend on transportation. Leave Los Angeles on day one and return on day six. Travel to San Diego, San Francisco, and Yosemite National Park. Make notes about each day, including your transportation and the costs.

	San Diego	San Francisco	Yosemite
Los Angeles	🚌 $40, 4 hours 🚆 $80, 3 hours ✈ $130, 1 hour	🚌 $60, 6 hours 🚆 $70, 8 hours ✈ $130, 1½ hours	🚌 $80, 7 hours 🚆 No service ✈ No service
San Diego		🚌 $135 round trip, 12 hours 🚆 No service ✈ $250, 1½ hours	🚌 $90, 10 hours 🚆 No service ✈ No service
San Francisco			🚌 $70, 4 hours 🚆 $60, 3 hours ✈ No service

2. Join another pair. Explain how you decided to spend your money.

D GOAL Plan How to Raise Money

Reading

A A charity is an organization that raises money to help people, animals, or the environment. Look at the logos for three charities and discuss the questions.

1. Do you know these charities? What do they do?

2. How do charities raise money?

B **MY WORLD** What charities are important in your country? What do they do?

C Read the first paragraph of the article. Check (✓) two sentences that are true about crowdfunding.

1. ☐ A lot of people give small amounts of money online.

2. ☐ It's only for people who want to start a business.

3. ☐ It can help musicians who want to make an album.

4. ☐ It's not very useful for charities.

D Read the rest of the article. What do these numbers refer to?

$125,000   65 feet   7,700 square miles $200

E Complete the chart. Use your notebook to write extra information.

	Problem	Action	Result
Sonam Wangchuk	People needed water.		
Size of Wales		It bought 7,700 square miles of rainforest.	
Watsi			People can pay for medical help.

✓ GOAL CHECK

In groups, plan how you will raise $1,000 for one of these charities:

- a group that gives free food to families in need
- a charity for dogs and cats that needs a new building
- a children's hospital that needs medical equipment

Plan how you will raise money. Design a poster for your charity. Present your ideas and poster to the class.

Crowdfunding for a Better World

"Crowdfunding" is a way of **raising money** from a large number of people on the internet. These days, there are a lot of different crowdfunding websites, but when crowdfunding began, it was mostly used by new businesses. Nowadays, people use it for a lot of different reasons, not just for business. For example, musicians who want to make an album can ask fans for money, a photographer can get money for a new book, and—increasingly—different types of charities raise money this way. Here are three examples of how crowdfunding has made a real difference in the world.

Bringing water

Sonam Wangchuk, an engineer, raised $125,000 on a crowdfunding site to build an "ice **stupa**." In higher parts of the Himalayas, the **glaciers** are disappearing, so local people have less water in the spring for growing crops. So, Sonam invented a way to bring water up the Himalayas in the winter from the lower parts of the mountains that have more water. As water comes out of a pipe, it freezes and becomes the 65-foot-tall ice stupa. Then, in the spring, the stupa **melts** and people have water for their fields.

Saving the rainforest

The organization "Size of Wales" wants to save rainforests because they are disappearing. It has already saved 7,700 square miles of rainforest (that's the same size as the country, Wales). Now it plans to save another 7,700. Crowdfunding is important for the organization because people give money, but it's also a good way to make people think about the problem of climate change.

Making people better

For people in poor countries, healthcare is very expensive. But the crowdfunding site Watsi has a solution. On the Watsi site, people describe their medical problems. For example, perhaps there's a farmer who needs $200 to pay for an operation on his mouth, or maybe there's a college student who can't hear. If she receives $400, she can pay for an operation on her ears. When people read about these individuals, they want to give them the money they need.

So if you want to give money to a charity, visit a crowdfunding site—or, if you want to raise money for a charity, why not try crowdfunding for yourself?

raise money get money from other people for a special reason (e.g., for a charity or a business)
stupa a religious tower in Buddhism
glacier a river of ice that moves slowly down a mountain
melt when ice becomes water

One of Sonam Wangchuk's ice stupas in Northwest India

E

GOAL Compare and Contrast Options

Communication

A **MY WORLD** We all have to make big decisions sometimes. What big decisions have you made? What big decisions do you think you will make in the future? Tell the class.

B In pairs, look at the list of life decisions. Discuss and rank them from 1 to 8 (1 = the most difficult decision, 8 = the easiest decision).

_____ moving to another country   _____ choosing a phone

_____ asking someone to marry you   _____ deciding what to wear to a party

_____ buying your first car   _____ buying a house

_____ applying for a job   _____ getting a student loan

C Work in groups. Three of your friends need to make big decisions. Discuss each situation and make a list of choices. Decide what your friend should do.

| 1. A friend works in a restaurant and he's a very good chef. He wants to open his own restaurant, but he needs money to start the business. He thinks he should ask his bank for a loan. What should he do? | 2. A friend works for a large company. The company wants her to work in another country for two years. She likes her job, but she also likes her home and her friends. What should she do? | 3. A friend won over $1,000 in the lottery. She is a student and never has much money. She also does volunteer work with a charity for animals. The charity always needs more money. What should she do? |

A woman cares for cats at a cat and dog rescue charity in Hiroshima, Japan.

If he asks for a loan, he'll pay interest.

But if she goes away, she won't be near her friends.

She should keep the money!

166 Unit 12

D Compare your decisions for each friend with another group.

Writing

E Read the email. Which of the three friends in **C** is this person writing to?

> Hi!
>
> It was great to hear your news! It's exciting, but you have a really difficult decision to make. On the one hand, moving to a new country is an amazing opportunity. If you live there, you'll learn a new language and see some amazing new places! On the other hand, you'll miss your family and friends.
>
> However, if you go, we'll all come and visit you! And also, it's only for two years. That isn't very long. So, overall, I think you should go!

F Read the information below and then underline the words for comparing and contrasting in the email in **E**.

WRITING SKILL: Compare and Contrast

When you compare and contrast different ideas and choices, you can use these linking words and phrases:
Describing similarities: *It also ... / In addition, ... / Similarly, ... / Both ...*
Comparing differences: *On the one hand, ... on the other hand, ... / However, ...*
/ In contrast ...
Concluding: *Overall, ... / On the whole, ... / I think ... / In conclusion, ...*

G Complete the sentences with words for comparing and contrasting.

1. _____ I think that doing volunteer work is the best choice.

2. On the one hand, going to the game would be fun, _____, I have a test tomorrow and need to study!

3. She needs a new car, so she should keep the money. _____, she also needs to pay for her classes soon.

 GOAL CHECK Compare and Contrast Options

1. Write an email to one of the other friends in **C**. Help your friend make a decision. Remember to use linking words and phrases to compare and contrast in your email.

2. Afterwards, exchange your emails in pairs. Do you think your partner gave good advice? Why?

VIDEO JOURNAL

HOW TO BUY HAPPINESS

Social scientist Michael Norton

A Read the list. Check the items under each question.

	Spent money on recently	Made you feel happy
1. Buying clothes	☐	☐
2. Meeting friends	☐	☐
3. Reading a book	☐	☐
4. Buying a present for someone else	☐	☐
5. Giving money to a charity	☐	☐
6. Buying jewelry	☐	☐
7. Going to a restaurant	☐	☐
8. Giving money to a homeless person	☐	☐

B In groups, compare your answers in **A**. Then discuss these questions:

1. When you spent money, did it make you happy?

2. Do you think money can buy you happiness?

C Watch the video of Michael Norton. Number information in the order you see or hear it.

_____ In 136 countries

_____ Money can't buy you happiness.

_____ Uganda

_____ By 5 p.m., spend this money on someone else.

_____ Money can buy you happiness if you spend it correctly.

_____ By 5 p.m., spend this money on yourself.

_____ Canada

_____ If you think money can't buy you happiness, give some of it away.

D Read the sentences about Michael's talk and underline the correct words. Then watch the talk again and check your answers.

1. Michael did an experiment with *two / three* groups of students.

2. The first group of students spent their money on *the same thing / different things*.

3. These students said it didn't make them *happy / less happy*.

4. Some members of the second group gave their money to people with no *home / money*.

5. Michael found that giving more money makes *a difference / no difference* to your happiness.

6. When you pay someone's medical bills and when you buy a present, the result is *the same / different*.

7. The poll of people in 136 countries shows that *most people feel / everyone feels* happier when they give money to charity.

E Complete these sentences with your own words. Then compare your ideas in groups.

1. The most interesting thing was that

_____

_____

2. One surprising thing was that

_____

_____

3. One question I would like to ask Michael is:

_____

_____

F In groups, write a questionnaire with six questions about money and happiness. Use ideas from Michael's talk and your own ideas.

G Take turns asking your questions with other groups. Then present your results to the class. What did you find out about your class?

A man gives money to a homeless person in London, England.

Grammar Reference

UNIT 1

Lesson A

Affirmative Statements with *Be*

Subject Pronoun + *Be*		*Be* Contractions*	
I **am**		I**'m**	
You **are** We **are** They **are**	Thai.	You**'re** We**'re** They**'re**	Thai.
He **is** She **is** It **is**		He**'s** She**'s** It**'s**	

*We use contractions for everyday speaking and writing.

Negative Statements with *Be*

Subject Pronoun + *be* + *not*			*be* + *not* Contractions	
I **am**		Mexican.	I**'m not**	
You **are** We **are** They **are**	**not**	teachers.	You **aren't** We **aren't** They **aren't**	Mexican.
He **is** She **is** It **is**		a teacher.	He **isn't** She **isn't** It **isn't**	

Yes / No Questions with *Be*

Be	Pronoun		Short Answers*
Are	you / we / they	Chinese?	Yes, I **am**. No, I**'m not**.
Is	he / she / it		Yes, they **are**. No, he **isn't**.

*Say: *Yes, I am; Yes, he is.* (don't say ~~Yes, I'm~~; ~~Yes, he's.~~)

A Underline the correct form of *be.*

1. I *am* / *is* a doctor.
2. She *'s* / *'re* a photographer.
3. Julia and Luis *am* / *are* from Brazil.
4. We *isn't* / *aren't* from Canada. We're from the US.
5. He *am not* / *is not* a travel agent.
6. Are you Japanese? Yes, I *am* / *are*.
7. Is she a dancer? No, she *aren't* / *isn't*.
8. *Are* / *Is* they from Australia?

B Fill in the blanks with a pronoun and the correct form of the verb *be.*

1. _____I'm not_____ from Japan. I'm from Thailand.
2. **A:** _____ from Indonesia? **B:** Yes, I am.
3. **A:** _____ a teacher? **B:** No, she isn't.
4. **A:** Where _____ from? **B:** They're from China.
5. _____ an engineer. He's a doctor.
6. **A:** Where _____ from? **B:** She's from France.
7. **A:** Is Lima a city in Chile? No, _____.
   B: It's in Peru.
8. **A:** _____ students? **B:** Yes, they are.

Lesson B

Wh- Questions with *Be*

What Where Who	is / ('s)	your name? your school? your teacher?
How old	are	your friends?

C Write the correct question word and form of *be.*

1. **A:** _____What's_____ your name? **B:** My name's Piotr.
2. **A:** _____ he from? **B:** Indonesia.
3. **A:** _____ your friend? **B:** She's 17.
4. **A:** _____ she? **B:** She's my sister.
5. **A:** _____ your job like?
   B: It's interesting.
6. **A:** _____ Gabriela's nationality?
   B: She's Costa Rican.
7. **A:** _____ your names?
   B: I'm Diego and this is Rita.

Lesson C

Be + Adjective

Subject	*be*	Adjective
My job	**is**	easy.
She	**'s**	interesting.
I	**'m not**	rich.
They	**are**	happy.

Be + Adjective + Noun

Singular				
Subject	*be*	Article	Adjective	Noun
It	**is**	an	easy	job.
She	**'s**	an	interesting	person.
I	**'m not**	a	rich	person.

Plural			
Subject	*be*	Adjective	Noun
They	**are**	easy	jobs.
We	**aren't**	rich	people.

D Underline the correct words to complete the sentence.

1. My job is <u>boring</u> / *a boring*.
2. English is *difficult* / *a difficult* language.
3. This photograph is *beautiful* / *a beautiful*.
4. Ricardo is *happy* / *a happy*!
5. Teaching isn't *easy* / *an easy* job.
6. My friend isn't *rich* / *a rich*.
7. I'm a police officer. Sometimes, it's *dangerous* / *a dangerous* job.
8. It's a job with *good* / *a good* salary.

E Complete the second sentence so it has the same meaning as the first.

1. Javier is unhappy.
   Javier _____ *is an unhappy* _____ man.
2. Peru is beautiful.
   Peru _____ country.
3. I'm a doctor. It's interesting.
   I'm a doctor. It _____ job.
4. This house is big.
   This _____ house.
5. The film is boring.
   It _____ film.
6. Frida and Bill are unhappy.
   Frida and Bill _____ people.

UNIT 2

Lesson A

Simple Present

We use the simple present to talk about:
- habits and routines: *I* **start** *work at nine o'clock.*
- things that are always true: *He* **lives** *in Singapore.*

Statements	Negative
I / You **live** in Beijing. Alison **catches** the bus at five thirty. We / They **go** to the movies every Saturday.	I / You **don't eat** breakfast. Alison **doesn't catch** the bus at six thirty. We / They **don't go** to the movies every Friday.

Yes / No Questions	Short Answers
Do you **live** in this city? **Does** Alison **catch** the bus at 5:30? **Do** we / they **go** to the movies on weekends?	Yes, I **do**. / No, I **don't**. Yes, she **does**. / No, she **doesn't**. Yes, they **do**. / No, they **don't**.

Wh- Questions	
Where **do** you **live**? When **do** you **catch** the bus? What time **does** he **finish** work?	In Bogotá. At 8:00. At 5:00.

Spelling rules with *he / she / it* + -s:
- Most verbs: *live → lives, start → starts, work → works*
- Verbs ending with -s, -sh, -ch, -o: *finish → finishes, watch → watches, go → goes*
- Verbs ending with consonant + y: *study → studies, fly → flies*
- Irregular verbs: *be → is, have → has*

A Underline the correct form of the verb.

1. He *live* / <u>lives</u> in Brasilia.
2. She *work* / *works* at a college.
3. I *get up* / *gets up* at seven o'clock.
4. Rafael and Magaly *go* / *goes* to the movies every Thursday night.
5. We *catch* / *catches* the bus to school.
6. The store *open* / *opens* at nine o'clock.
7. I *don't drink* / *doesn't drink* tea or coffee.
8. Chen *don't play* / *doesn't play* the piano.

B Match the questions to the answers.

1. What do you do? __c__
2. Do you live in Tokyo? _____
3. Where do you study English? _____
4. Does Eric work here? _____
5. What time does Helen catch the bus? _____
6. Do they watch TV? _____

a. Yes, he does.
b. No, they don't.
c. I work in a bank.
d. At a language school.
e. No, I don't. I live in Kyoto.
f. At twelve o'clock.

C Write the *he / she / it* form of these verbs.

1. watch <u>watches</u>
2. do _____
3. drive _____
4. take _____
5. teach _____
6. play _____
7. marry _____
8. make _____
9. go _____
10. dance _____

Lesson C

Adverb of Frequency + Verb

We use adverbs of frequency to say how often we do something:

100%

*I **always** get up at seven o'clock.*

*He **usually** takes the bus to work.*

*You **often** go to the movies on weekends.*

*She **sometimes** eats out in the evening.*

*We **don't often** / **don't usually** have parties.*

*They **never** finish work at five.*

0%

Word Order			
Subject	Adverb of Frequency	Verb	
We	**always**	give	presents at Christmas.
We	**never**	dance	in the streets at Christmas.
Subject	*Be*	Adverb of Frequency	
Christmas	is	**always**	in December.
Carnival	is	**usually**	in March.
Most adverbs of frequency come before the verb, unless the verb is *be*.			

D Look at the table and write sentences with the adverbs of frequency.

	Movies	Park
Sam	sometimes	never
Jane	always	often
Carlo and Donna	not often	sometimes

1. Sam / movies ___Sam sometimes goes to the movies.___
2. Carlo and Donna / the park _____
   _____
3. Jane / movies _____
4. Carlo and Donna / movies _____
   _____
5. Jane / park _____
6. Sam / park _____

E Check (✓) the sentences with the correct word order. Rewrite the other sentences.

1. We always celebrate Thanksgiving in November. ✓
2. I go never to the park. ✗ *I never go to the park.*
3. They don't start often work at nine.
4. He sometimes finishes early.
5. Kim and Mai often speak English together.
6. I watch TV always in the evening.
7. Sue doesn't often catch the bus to work.
8. My brother remembers never my birthday.

UNIT 3

Lesson A

Possession				
's	Adjective*	Pronoun	*belong to*	
	my	**mine**		me.
	your	**yours**		you.
It's Tim**'s** passport.	**his**	**his**		him.
It's my sister**'s** bag.	**her**	**hers**	It **belongs to** They **belong to**	her.
	our	**ours**		us.
It's my parent**s'** bag.	**their**	**theirs**		them.
*A possessive adjective has one form for singular and plural: *his ticket, his tickets*				

A Underline the correct word.

1. It's *my* / *mine* / *me* passport.
2. These keys are *you* / *your* / *yours*.
3. This car belongs to *my* / *me* / *mine*.
4. Is this *he* / *his* / *him* ticket?
5. These bags are *their* / *theirs* / *them*.
6. Does this camera belong to *she* / *her* / *hers*?
7. These books are *our* / *ours* / *us*.
8. This watch belongs to *me* / *my* / *mine*.
9. They belong to *us* / *our* / *ours*.
10. Is this *you* / *your* / *yours* luggage?

B Write the missing words in these conversations.

1. **A:** Whose passport is this?
   B: I think it's Joe _____, but look at the photo.
   A: No, it isn't _____ because it's a woman's face.

2. A: I like your bag.

   B: It's my sister _____ bag.

   A: Does the camera belong to _____, too?

   B: No, it belongs to me. It's _____.

3. A: Excuse me, I think you're in _____ seat.

   B: Are you sure? I think it's _____.

   A: I'm in seat 30 C.

   B: This is seat 29 C. _____ is behind me.

Lesson C

Should for Advice

You	**should** **shouldn't**	buy	this coat.

Use *should* for strong advice. *Should* is a modal verb: Do not use third person *-s*: *You should buy it.* / ~~You shoulds buy it.~~ Do not use *do* in negatives: *You shouldn't buy it.* / ~~You don't should buy it.~~

Yes / No Questions and Short Answers

Should	I	take	a taxi?	Yes, you **should**. No, you **shouldn't**.

Wh- Questions

What	**should**	I	do?

C Write *should* or *shouldn't*.

1. You _____ take sunblock to the beach.

2. You _____ eat healthy food.

3. You _____ smoke cigarettes.

4. A: I'm tired.

   B: You _____ get more sleep.

5. A: Should I take a taxi?

   B: No, you _____. It's expensive.

D Give advice. Use *should / shouldn't buy* and *it* or *them*.

1. This coat is beautiful. *You should buy it.*

2. This camera is very expensive. _____

3. These shoes are nice. _____

4. These shirts are ugly! _____

5. This phone is fantastic! _____

6. This laptop is slow. _____

E Match the questions to the answers.

1. Should I go to the gym? _____

2. Should we go now? _____

3. I'm sick. What should I do? _____

a. No, the movie starts later.

b. You should see a doctor.

c. Yes, you should. Exercise is good for you.

UNIT 4

Lesson A

Count and Non-Count Nouns

There are two types of nouns:

- Count nouns (you can count them): *1 apple, 2 apples, 3 apples …*
- Non-count nouns (you cannot count them): *bread, juice, cheese …*

	Singular	Plural
Count nouns	This is a banana.	These are bananas.
Non-count nouns	This is water.	~~These are waters.~~

For regular count nouns, add *-s* or *-es* to form the plural. Non-count nouns do not have a plural form.

a / an, some, and *any*

	Count nouns		Non-count nouns
	Singular	Plural	
Statement	It's **a** lemon.	There are **some** eggs in the fridge.	There is **some** cheese in the fridge.
Negative	I don't have **an** egg.	There aren't **any** eggs in the fridge.	I don't have **any** milk.
Question	Do you have **an** orange?	Are there **any** apples?	Do you have **any** orange juice?

a / an

Use *a / an* with singular count nouns: *a lemon, an egg*.

Use *a* before a noun with a consonant sound: *a potato, a banana*.

Use *an* before a noun with a vowel sound: *an orange, an apple*.

some

Use *some* in affirmative statements with plural count nouns and non-count nouns:

I have some eggs. / *You have some cheese.*

You can also use *some* for questions with *could*: *Could I have some milk?*

any

Use *any* with count nouns and non-count nouns in:

- Negative statements: *There aren't **any** bananas. / I don't have **any** butter.*
- Questions: *Are there **any** bananas? Do you have **any** butter?*

A Cross out one incorrect word in each group of count nouns or non-count nouns.

1. apple / orange / banana / ~~milk~~
2. juice / bread / eggs / water
3. tea / tomato / lemon / sausage
4. banana / butter / onion / hamburger
5. salad / orange / water / coffee

B Match the two halves of the sentences.

1. I have an _____
2. There's a _____
3. There aren't any _____
4. We don't have _____
5. Do you have _____
6. Are there any _____

a. any rice?   d. apple in my bag.
b. potatoes at the store.   e. any olive oil.
c. eggs in the fridge?   f. steak in the fridge.

C Complete the sentences with *a / an*, *some*, or *any*.

1. Do we have _____ tomatoes?
2. Pass me _____ apples, please.
3. We need _____ onion.
4. I think there is _____ cheese on the table.
5. There aren't _____ eggs.
6. Could I have _____ water, please?
7. There isn't _____ juice in the bottle.
8. Do you have _____ banana?
9. Would you like _____ salt?

Lesson C

How much and How many with Quantifiers

Information Questions		Quantifiers		
		++++	+	–
Count Nouns	**How many** oranges do you need?	I need **lots of / a lot of** oranges.	I need **a few** oranges.	I **don't** need **many** oranges.

Non-count Nouns	**How much** bread do we have?	We have **lots of / a lot of** bread.	We have **a little** bread.	We **don't** have **much** bread.

With count nouns, ask about quantities with *How many... ?* With non-count nouns, ask about quantities with *How much... ?*
Use *a lot of / lots of* to talk about large quantities with count and non-count nouns. *A lot of* is slightly more common in American English. *Lots of* is more common in British English.
Use *a few* and *not many* to talk about small quantities with count nouns.
Use *a little* and *not much* to talk about small quantities with non-count nouns.

For short answers, say: *a few, a little, not many, not much.*

How many do you need? **A few.**
How much do we have? **A little.**

With short answers, you can also say *A lot* (not ~~Lots of~~) with count or non-count noun questions:

How many do you need? **A lot.**
How much do we have? **A lot.**

D Complete the sentences using *a little* or *a few*.

1. There is only _____ tuna salad in the fridge.
2. We only need _____ apples.
3. Please bring _____ bananas.
4. I only take _____ sugar in my coffee.
5. There are just _____ sausages left.
6. **A:** How many onions do you have?
   B: _____.
7. **A:** How much soup is there?
   B: _____.

E Write the opposite sentence using the word in parentheses.

1. There are a lot of potatoes on the table. (many)
   There aren't many potatoes on the table.
2. There are a lot of potatoes on the table. (few)
   _____
3. I have a little water in my bottle. (lots)
   _____
4. There's a lot of cheese in this package. (little)
   _____
5. We need a lot of broccoli for dinner. (much)
   _____

F Write in the missing words.

1. **A:** How _____ do you want?
   B: Just a little.

2. **A:** How many lemons do we need?
   B: It's a big party, so we need _____ of them.

3. **A:** How _____ cookies are there?
   B: Not many. Just a _____ at the bottom of the box.

4. **A:** How much juice do I need to buy?
   B: Only a _____.

UNIT 5

Lesson A
Present Continuous

Form the present continuous with *to be* + verb + *-ing*. We use the present continuous to talk about things that are happening now (or around the time of speaking).

Affirmative and Negative Statements

I	**am ('m)** **am** not (**'m** not)	
He / She / It	**is ('s)** **is** not (**is**n't)	**playing** soccer (now).
You / We / They	**are ('re)** **are** not (**are**n't)	

Yes / No Questions

Am	I	
Are	you / we / they	**playing** soccer?
Is	he / she / it	

Short Answers

Affirmative		
	I	**am**.
Yes,	he / she / it	**is**.
	you / we / they	**are**.

Negative		
	I	**'m not**.
No,	he / she / it	**isn't**.
	you / we / they	**aren't**.

Wh- Questions

What	**am**	I	**doing**?
Where	**is**	he / she / it	**going**?
How long	**are**	you / we / they	**staying**?

Spelling rules:

Add *-ing* to most verbs: *play → playing, do → doing*

With verbs ending with a consonant + e, drop the e before adding *-ing*: *have → having, come → coming*

Double the final consonant for verbs that end in consonant-vowel-consonant (not including verbs ending in *-w, -x,* or *-y*): *sit → sitting*

A Write complete sentences using the present continuous.

1. They / play / baseball / now. <u>They're playing baseball now.</u>
2. I / not / study / today. _____
3. It / rain / outside. _____
4. We / not / do / any exercise.
   _____
5. Sarah / climb / and / hike / in the mountains.
   _____
6. My family / go / on vacation / this morning.
   _____
7. Barcelona / play / against Real Madrid today.
   _____
8. I / do / yoga. _____

B Match the questions to the answers.

1. Are you working today? _____
2. Is he driving to your house? _____
3. What are Peter and Sue doing? _____
4. Where are you walking? _____
5. Are we meeting in this room? _____
6. What are you watching? _____

a. No, he isn't. He's taking the bus.
b. In Yosemite park. It's beautiful!
c. I think they're studying today.
d. Yes, we are. Let's go in.
e. Basketball.
f. No, I'm not. I have a day off.

Simple Present and Present Continuous

Use the simple present to talk about:

- Habits and routines: *I **play** soccer once a week.*
- Things that are true all the time: *In soccer, each team **has** 11 players.*

Use the present continuous to talk about:

- Things that are happening now or at the moment of speaking: *I**'m studying** English (at the moment).*
- Things that are happening around the time of speaking or temporary situations: *I**'m working** for a company in London.*

C Write the verbs in parentheses in the simple present or the present continuous.

Helen: Hi, Chen. It's Helen. I (1) _____ (call) from the gym.

Chen: What sports (2) _____ (you / do) there?

Helen: I (3) _____ (not / do) anything at the moment. I (4) _____ (eat) lunch in the cafe! Meet me here!

Chen: Sorry, but Jill and I (5) _____ (play) tennis. We're at the park now.

Helen: But you usually (6) _____ (play) tennis on Tuesdays.

Chen: I know, but Jill (7) _____ (have) a new job and she (8) _____ (work) on Tuesdays.

Lesson C

Stative Verbs			
like	Why do you **like** outdoor sports?	know	You **know** I can't swim.
hate	I **hate** indoor sports.	want	I don't **want** to go bungee jumping.
think	I **think** indoor sports are boring.	need	You **need** a lot of equipment.
prefer	Do you **prefer** outdoor sports?	cost	The equipment **costs** a lot of money.
Stative verbs refer to states, thoughts, and feelings. We don't often use them with the present continuous: *I love tennis. ~~I'm loving tennis.~~* *I don't understand the answer to this question. ~~I'm not understanding the answer to this question.~~* *I hate outdoor sports. ~~I am hating outdoor sports.~~*			

D Underline the correct verb in these sentences.

1. Skiing *costs / is costing* a lot of money.
2. The children *need / are needing* new soccer shirts.
3. Roger and Christine *play / are playing* in the yard right now.
4. I don't like team games. I *prefer / am preferring* individual sports.
5. Ashira *doesn't like / is not liking* to go swimming.
6. We *go / are going* hiking. Can I call you back?
7. I like rock climbing, but my friend *hates / is hating* it.
8. Frederick can't come. He *does / is doing* his homework.

UNIT 6

Lesson A

Simple Past		
I / You / He / She / It / We / They	**worked lived**	in Singapore in 2018.
Use the simple past to talk about finished actions and events. Add -ed to regular verbs to form the simple past.		

Regular verbs include:

arrive – arrived	pack – packed
ask – asked	play – played
change – changed	relax – relaxed
help – helped	return – returned
learn – learned	stay – stayed
like – liked	travel – traveled
love – loved	visit – visited
need – needed	want – wanted

Spelling rules:

Add -ed to most verbs. There are some exceptions:

- Two syllable verbs ending with -y: *study – studied* (not ~~studyed~~)
- Verbs ending with -e: *like – liked, live – lived*
- Double the last consonant with verbs ending in a vowel + a consonant: *stop – stopped*

Some verbs are irregular (such as *go* and *fly*). Do not add -ed.

I / You / He / She / It / We / They	**went flew**	to Singapore in 2018.

Other irregular verbs include:

buy – bought	pay – paid
drink – drank	say – said
eat – ate	see – saw
find – found	spend – spent
have – had	take – took
know – knew	tell – told
leave – left	think – thought

Negative			
I	**didn't**	**live**	in Singapore.
		go	to Hanoi.

Yes / No Questions				Answers
Did	I / you / he / she / it / we / they	**live**	there?	Yes, we **did**.
		go		No, we **didn't**.

Information Questions				
Where				To Cancun.
How long	**did** you **go**	on vacation last year?		For 2 weeks.
When				In the summer.

A Complete the travel diary. Write the simple past of the words in parentheses.

Day 1 _Arrived_ (arrive) in Dar es Salaam. _____ (check) into hotel. _____ (unpack) suitcases. Went swimming.

Day 2 _____ (take) boat to the island of Zanzibar.

Days 3–5 _____ (sunbathe) on the beach. _____ (go) diving.

Day 6 _____ (fly) to Arusha. Saw Kilimanjaro. It's BIG!

Days 7–10 _____ (take) a safari tour. _____ (see) hundreds of wild animals. Took lots of photos.

Day 11 _____ (return) to Arusha. _____ (buy) souvenirs. Took plane to Dar es Salaam and then flew home. Great trip!

B 🎧 29 Complete the questions for these answers. Then listen and check your answers.

1. **A:** When ___ _did you go to_ ___ Beijing?
   B: We went to Beijing in 2015.

2. **A:** How long _____ at the hotel?
   B: I stayed at the hotel for 2 weeks.

3. **A:** _____ your friends?
   B: No, I didn't visit my friends. I visited my family.

4. **A:** _____ to?
   B: We flew to Hanoi.

5. **A:** _____ good time?
   B: Yes, I did. I had a really good time.

Lesson C

Simple Past of *to be*		
Affirmative		
I / He / She / It	**was**	tired last night.
You / We / They	**were**	
Use *was* / *were* to talk about the past: I am / He is → I **was** / He **was** They are → They **were**		

Negative		
I / He / She / It	**wasn't**	tired last night.
You / We / They	**weren't**	

Yes / No Questions			Short Answers
Was	I / he / she / it	tired last night?	Yes, I **was**. / No, I **wasn't**.
Were	you / we / they		Yes, we **were**. / No, they **weren't**.

Information Questions			Answers
How	**was**	your weekend?	It **was** great!
Why	**were**	you late?	I **was** busy at work.

C Underline *was* or *were* to complete the sentences.

1. We didn't enjoy the vacation. The weather *was* / *were* very bad.

2. How *was* / *were* the food?

3. *Was* / *Were* you tired when you got home?

4. We *was* / *were* really interested in the ruins. They *was* / *were* amazing.

5. *Was* / *Were* the hotels clean?

6. Why *was* / *were* your flight late?

D Write the correct form of *be*.

A: How (1) _____ your vacation?

B: It (2) _____ OK, but we had some problems.

A: Why? What happened?

B: We went with a tour, but our tour guide (3) _____ very good. He didn't know anything about history. Also, the seats on the bus (4) _____ very comfortable. Next time I want to go by train!

A: What (5) _____ your favorite city?

B: Venice (6) _____ beautiful, but there (7) _____ thousands of other tourists.

A: (8) _____ the hotels comfortable?

B: Yes, they (9) _____. I liked all the hotels!

UNIT 7

Lesson A

Verbs with Direct and Indirect Objects			
Subject	Verb	Indirect Object	Direct Object
Rose	sent	Jim	an email.
They	bought	me	a smartphone.
I	am writing	Helen	a text message.
	Find	me	his number, please.
My boss	didn't email	her	the report.
	Give	me	a call.

A Write the missing words in this conversation.

didn't send   email   me   money   sent   you

Ken: Hey, Chris. I (1) _____ you an
(2) _____ yesterday and you
didn't answer.

Chris: Email? What email? You didn't send
(3) _____ an email.

Ken: Well, I also sent (4) _____ a text
message.

Chris: Text message? What text message? You
(5) _____ me a text message,
either. Really!

Ken: I'm sure I did! Anyway, where's the
(6) _____ you owe me?

Chris: Money? What money?

B Match the two halves of the sentences.

1. I emailed _____
2. They didn't _____
3. Please send _____
4. I'm sending her _____
5. Her friend didn't buy
_____

a. text me the plans.
b. me your phone number.
c. the address.
d. you my number.
e. her a present.

Lesson C

Sensory Verbs

Subject	Verb	Adjective
The food	smells	delicious.
It	feels	soft.
You	look	cold.
It	tastes	salty.
He	sounds	tired.

Sensory verbs are stative verbs (see page 176).
They are not usually used in the present continuous:
The food smells delicious. The food is smelling delicious.
They are usually followed by an adjective:
*The food smells **delicious**. / It feels **soft**.*

C Complete the sentences about the photos with the words in the box.

awful   dirty   green   loud   salty   soft   sweet   wet

1. Those taste _____*sweet*_____. Try one!
2. That sounds too _____. Turn it down!
3. This feels _____.

4. Those look _____, but some are darker
than others.
5. They look _____.
6. That smells _____. I don't like it.
7. Pretzels taste _____.
8. After all the rain today, I feel _____!

1	2

3	4

5	6

7	8

D Complete the sentences with sensory verbs.

1. I don't _____ well today. I need a
doctor.
2. How does that singer _____ so young?
He's 75 years old!
3. Add some chili, so it _____ hotter.
4. Your new aftershave _____ wonderful.
5. Thanks for the massage. My back
_____ great now.
6. **A:** Does it _____ OK?
B: Delicious, thanks. Did you cook it?

UNIT 8

Lesson A

Future: *be going to*				
Statements				
I	am 'm	going to	buy a new car. get a job. clean the house.	
He She It	is 's			
You We They	are 're			
Use *be going to* to talk about plans for the future.				

Negatives				
I	am not 'm not	going to	get married. do the laundry. take a vacation.	
He She It	is not isn't			
You We They	are not aren't			

Yes / No Questions				Short Answers
Are	you	**going to**	take a vacation?	Yes, I **am**. / No, I**'m not**. Yes, he **is**. / No, he **isn't**.
Is	he			

Wh- Questions	Answers
When are you going to do the laundry? **Where** are you going to get a job?	Tomorrow. At this store.
We often use *be going to* with these time expressions: *tomorrow, next Sunday / week / year.*	

A Match the questions and the answers.

1. Where are you going to have lunch today? _____
2. Are you going to invite Ajay to the party? _____
3. What are you going to do on Saturday? _____
4. When is Nicola going to arrive? _____
5. Is it going to rain tonight? _____

a. Yes, I am. He loves dancing.
b. Maybe. You should take an umbrella.
c. At Luigi's
d. We're going to go ice skating.
e. Her plane arrives at five o'clock.

B Complete the conversation with *be going to* and the verbs in parentheses.

A: Hey! I just won $100!
B: Wow! What (1) _____ (you / do) with it?
A: Well, first, I (2) _____ (buy) my mother some flowers.
B: Great. She (3) _____ (love) those.
A: And then, I (4) _____ (give) my sister $10.
B: And the rest?
A: I (5) _____ (put) it in the bank.
B: (6) _____ (you / buy) anything for yourself?
A: Maybe. But not now.

Lesson C

Will			
Statements and Negatives			
I / You / He / She / It / We / They	**will ('ll)**	be	an astronaut some day.
	will not (won't)		
Use *will* + verb to make predictions about the future.			

Yes / No Questions				Short Answers
Will	I / you / he / she / it / we / they	be	famous?	Yes, I **will**. / No, I **won't**.

C Complete the sentences with *will* or *won't* and a verb from the box.

be	become	drive	get	have

1. They work hard, so I think they _____*'ll be*_____ rich one day.
2. Everyone _____ electric cars by 2050.
3. Humans _____ any oil in the future.
4. _____ I _____ a prize if I win the game?
5. You _____ a scientist, but I think you'll be a science teacher.

Will and *be going to*

We can use *will* and *be going to* to talk about future predictions. While *going to* was traditionally used to talk about plans and *will* was traditionally used to talk about predictions, there is little or no difference in meaning.

D Rewrite the questions using *be going to* or *will*.

be going to	will
1. Is it going to rain tomorrow?	
2.	Will it be sunny this afternoon?
3. Are we going to have a hot summer this year?	
4.	What will the weather be like this weekend?
5. Is it going to be cloudy tomorrow?	
6.	Will we finish the book before the end of the year?
7. Are temperatures going to rise in the next 100 years?	
8.	Will you get good grades?

Will + Adverb of Certainty

We often use the adverbs *certainly, definitely, probably,* and *possibly* with *will* for predictions. These adverbs say if the speaker is more or less certain of something.

100% ▲	I**'ll definitely** / **certainly** be happy.
	I**'ll probably** live to be 100.
50%	I**'ll possibly** be famous.
	I **probably won't** go out tomorrow night.
0% ▼	I **definitely won't** speak perfect English.

Note the word order:

(1) *will* + adverb

Robots **will definitely** / **certainly** *do housework in the future.*

Cars **will probably** *fly in the future.*

(2) adverb + *won't*

Humans **probably won't** *watch TV in 2050.*

I **definitely won't** *travel into space.*

E Put the adverb in the correct position.
1. We will ˄certainly travel to Mars by 2030. (certainly)
2. Humans won't drive cars in the 22nd century. (definitely)
3. My brother will become a famous singer. (possibly)
4. I won't pass the test. (probably)

UNIT 9

Lesson A
Comparatives

Change an adjective into the comparative form to compare two things:

Your car is **faster than** *mine.*

These socks are **smaller than** *those ones.*

This book is **more interesting than** *my last one.*

My phone is **better than** *yours.*

The comparative form is often followed by *than*. You can also add *much* to make the comparison stronger:

These socks are **much smaller than** *those ones.*

My phone is **much better than** *yours.*

Regular Adjectives	
Adjective	Comparative
cheap	cheaper
fast	faster
beautiful	more beautiful
fashionable	more fashionable

Spelling rules:
- Add *-er* to short adjectives to form the comparative: *young – young**er***
- When the adjective ends in *-e*, add *-r*: *large – large**r***
- Change adjectives ending in *-y* (after a consonant) to *-i*: *happy – happ**ier***
- Double the final consonant on some adjectives ending with a vowel and a consonant: *hot – hot**ter**, big – big**ger***
- Add *more* or *less* before adjectives with two or more syllables: *interesting – more / less interesting*

Irregular Adjectives	
Adjective	Comparative
good	better
bad	worse

A Complete the conversation with the comparative form of the adjectives in parentheses.

A: I like your new car. Was it expensive?

B: No, it was (1) _____ (cheap) than my old car. But it's much (2) _____ (fast)!

A: Can I sit in it?

B: Sure!

A: Oh, it's (3) _____ (comfortable) than your other car, too. It also feels (4) _____ (big) inside.

B: Yes, I think it is. The design is much (5) _____ (good).

B Make comparative sentences.

1. This motorcycle / fast / than / your car.
   This motorcycle is faster than your car.

2. My brother / tall / you.
   _____

3. The Amazon River / long / the Ganges River.
   _____

4. Your apartment / much / big / mine.
   _____

Lesson C
Superlatives

Change an adjective into the superlative form to compare three or more things. Use *the* before the superlative form:

*Your car is **the fastest**.*

*These socks are **the smallest**.*

*This book is **the most interesting**.*

*My phone is **the best**.*

Regular Adjectives

Adjective	Superlative
cheap	the cheapest
fast	the fastest
beautiful	the most beautiful
fashionable	the most fashionable

Spelling rules:

- Add -*est* to short adjectives to form the comparative: *young – young**est***

- When the adjective ends in -*e*, add -*st*: *large – large**st***

- Change adjectives ending in -*y* (after a consonant) to -*i*: *happy – happ**iest***

- Double the final consonant on adjectives ending with a vowel and a consonant: *hot – hot**test**, big – big**gest***

- Add *most* or *least* before adjectives with two or more syllables: *beautiful – the **most** / **least** beautiful*

Irregular Adjectives

Adjective	Superlative
good	best
bad	worst

C Complete the sentences with the superlative form of the adjectives in parentheses.

1. Mount Everest is ___*the highest*___ (high) mountain in the world.

2. Mexican food is hotter than Chinese food, but Indian food is _____. (hot)

3. Which one is _____ (cheap)?

4. I like a lot of European cities, but Paris is _____ (beautiful).

5. Elephants are heavy, but blue whales are _____ (heavy) animals in the world.

6. I think I'm _____ (bad) math student in my class.

7. Cotton is cheaper than silk, but polyester is _____ (cheap) material.

8. I like those two sweaters, but this one is _____ (warm).

D Add the missing adjectives, comparatives, or superlatives to the table.

Adjective	Comparative	Superlative
slow	slower	slowest
short	1.	shortest
2.	bigger	3.
4.	5.	heaviest
dangerous	6.	7.
8.	better	9.
bad	10.	11.

E Write the missing letters to complete the words. Some are comparatives and some are superlatives.

1. My sister is old_____ than me.
2. I'm the old_____ student in my class.
3. New York is big_____ than San Francisco.
4. I think my grandfather is the happ_____ person in the world!
5. This movie is funn_____ than the other one.
6. That cafe serves the wors_____ food in the world! It's horrible.

UNIT 10

Lesson A

Modals (*could, should, must*); *have to*

You can use the modal verbs *could*, *should*, *must*, and the verb *have to* to give advice.

- Make suggestions and give gentle advice with *could*: You **could** *turn the TV off and go outside.*
- Give strong advice with *should* or *shouldn't*: You **should** *run a marathon.* / You **shouldn't** *drive so fast.*
- Sometimes we also use *ought to* for giving strong advice: You **ought to** *run a marathon.* / You **ought not to** *run a marathon.* The negative is *ought not to*. It is very uncommon in American English.
- Express obligation and give very strong advice with *must* or *have to*: You **must** *drink more water!* You **have to** *drink more water!*

Could, *should*, *ought to*, and *must* are modal verbs. With modal verbs:

- Don't use a third person *-s*: You should go. ~~You shoulds go.~~
- Don't use the auxiliary *do*: I couldn't go. ~~I don't could go.~~
- Don't use *to* before the next verb (except with *ought to*): You should get exercise. ~~You should to get exercise.~~

Have to is not a modal verb, but it has a similar meaning to *must* when we give advice:

You have to stop smoking. = You must stop smoking.

A Check (✓) the correct sentences. Rewrite the incorrect sentences (✗).

1. You should go on a diet. ✓
2. ~~She musts go to bed early.~~ ✗ *She must go to bed early.*
3. You don't should take the day off.
4. Bill should go by bus.
5. You could to get a new job.
6. Sally must stop sunbathing.
7. My father should to stop eating junk food.
8. Alicia has to work harder.

B Read each comment and complete the advice with a verb and your own words.

1. I work very long hours.
   You *could say "no" to your boss more often.* (gentle advice)
2. I always go to bed late.
   You _____
   _____. (strong advice)
3. I never get 100% on tests at school.
   You _____
   _____. (very strong advice)
4. I want to have fun this weekend.
   You _____
   _____. (gentle advice)

5. I don't eat any fruit or vegetables.
   You _____
   _____. (strong advice)
6. I want a better car.
   You _____
   _____. (very strong advice)

Lesson C
Questions with *How*

You can ask questions with *How* for different reasons.

How much / How many

- Use *how much* to ask about the quantity of non-count nouns: **How much** *water is there?* **How much** *do you weigh?*
- Use *how many* to ask about the quantity of count nouns: **How many** *people live in this house?* **How many** *apples do you want?*

How + Adjective

- Use *how old* to ask about age: **How old** *are you?* **How old** *is this car?*
- Use *how long* to ask about length or a period of time: **How long** *is the movie?* **How long** *are you staying at the hotel?*
- Use *how tall* to ask about human height or *how high* for the height of objects: **How tall** *are you?* **How high** *is Mount Everest?*
- Use *how big* to ask about size: **How big** *is your house?*
- Use *how far* to ask about distance: **How far** *is it from Shanghai to Bangkok?*

How often

Use *how often* to ask about frequency: **How often** *do you go to the movies?* **How often** *is there a train to Kyoto?*

How

Ask about the way you do something with *How*:

A: How *do you get downtown?*
B: *Go straight down this street.*
A: How *does this photocopier work?*
B: *Press the green button.*

Ask everyday questions with *How*:

A: How *are you?*
B: *Fine thanks.*
A: How *about a coffee?*
B: *No, thanks. I already had one.*

A: **How** was your weekend?
B: Great, thanks.

C Write the missing word to complete the questions.
1. **A:** How _____ is that building?
   B: It's about one hundred years old.
2. **A:** How _____ do you play tennis?
   B: About twice a week.
3. **A:** How _____ sugar do you want?
   B: A pound, please.
4. **A:** How _____ are you?
   B: About six feet tall.
5. **A:** How _____ is it from Hanoi to Ho Chi Minh City?
   B: About 1,100 miles.
6. **A:** How _____ students are in your class?
   B: Twenty.

D Reorder the words and add *How* to make questions.
1. was vacation your? _____ *How was your vacation?*
2. go often they do cycling? _____
3. your is big office? _____
4. is in the fridge much milk? _____
5. this turn on does? _____
6. the city center is far? _____
7. oranges do want many you? _____
8. you travel do to London? _____

UNIT 11

Lesson A

Present Perfect	
Statement	I **have finished** my homework. / He **has finished** his homework.
Negative	I **haven't finished**. / She **hasn't finished**.
Yes / No Questions	**Have** you **finished** your homework? / **Has** he **finished**? **Have** you **left** work? / **Has** she **left** work?
Short Answers	Yes, **I have**. / Yes, he **has**. No, **I haven't**. / No, she **hasn't**.
Wh- Questions	What **have** you **done** today? Where **has** she **been**? How long **have** they **known**?

Form the present perfect with *has / have* + past participle. We can use the present perfect (like the simple past) to talk about completed actions in the past, but without saying when they happened.

Past Participles

Regular verbs end in *-ed*:
walk – walked, clean – cleaned, pass – passed, graduate – graduated, visit – visited

Irregular verbs have irregular past participles:
cut – cut, buy – bought, have – had, go – gone, be – been, take – taken, pay – paid, put – put

A Write the irregular past participles from the box next to the correct verb.

read	spoken	drunk	bought	swept	told
won	said	made	eaten	met	done

1. buy _____
2. do _____
3. drink _____
4. eat _____
5. make _____
6. meet _____
7. read _____
8. say _____
9. speak _____
10. sweep _____
11. tell _____
12. win _____

B Complete the conversation with the present perfect.

1. **A:** What (1) _____ (you, do) today?
   B: Nothing very exciting. I (2) _____ (clean) the house, and I (3) _____ (cook) dinner. (4) _____ (you, have) an interesting day?
   A: No, not really. (5) _____ (I, be) sick. I (6) _____ (not do) anything.
2. **A:** Today, I (1) _____ (pay the bills) and I (2) _____ (buy the groceries). (3) _____ (you, have) an interesting day?
   B: Well, I (4) _____ (visit) a friend. And I (5) _____ (buy) some clothes for my new job.

Lesson C
Present Perfect vs Simple Past

Use the **present perfect** to talk about an action in the past when you don't know (or say) when the action happened: *Claudio has been to many countries.*

Use the **simple past** to talk about an action in the past when you know (and say) when the action happened: *Claudio went to Thailand yesterday.*

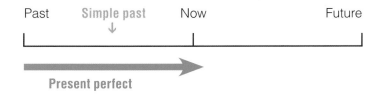

Past	Simple past	Now	Future
	↓		

Present perfect

Present Perfect *Have you ever* Questions

We often ask *Have you ever* questions to ask about life experiences:
Have you ever been to Thailand?

For negative answers, use *never*:
No, I've never been to Thailand.

With the simple past, we often use these time expressions: *yesterday, last week / month / year, in 2010*:
They **went** to Thailand **last year**.
Did he go to Thailand **last year**?

C Complete the sentences with the correct form of the verb in parentheses.

1. Last summer, we _____ (go) to the Maldives.
2. I _____ (live) in the same house all my life.
3. John _____ (never travel) abroad.
4. Spain _____ (win) the World Cup in 2010.
5. Brazil _____ (win) the World Cup five times.

D Complete the conversations with the correct form of the verbs in parentheses.

1. **A:** _____ (you / pass) your driving test?
   B: Yes. I _____ (take) it in January, and I _____ (pass) the first time.
2. **A:** _____ (you / be) to Europe?
   B: Yes, I have. I _____ (go) to Germany last year.

UNIT 12

Lesson A

Real Conditionals: The Zero Conditional	
If Clause (Simple Present)	Main Clause (Simple Present or Imperative)
If you **have** a loan,	you **pay** interest.
If you **borrow** money,	**remember** to pay it back.

We use the zero conditional to:
- talk about facts: *If you throw a ball up, it comes down.*
- talk about things that are usually true: *If there are clouds, it often rains.*
- give instructions: *If you press this button, your laptop starts.*
- give advice: *If you don't understand a word, ask your teacher.*

With the zero conditional, you can start with the *if* clause or the main clause.
If you have a loan, you pay interest. = You pay interest if you have a loan.

Punctuation

If you start with the *if* clause, put a comma after it: *If you need help, ask your teacher.*
If you start with the main clause, don't use a comma: *Ask your teacher if you need help.*

A Complete the rules with the words in the box.

> ask a friend   finish it on time   if you have a question
> if you work with a partner   learn from it
> leave the classroom   listen!

1. If your teacher speaks, _____
2. If you have homework, _____
3. If you don't know the answer to a question, _____
4. Try to use English _____
5. If you make a mistake, _____
6. Raise your hand _____
7. If the bell rings, _____

B Write sentences with the zero conditional.

1. traffic light / red / not drive
   If the traffic light is red, do not drive.
2. you heat ice / melts
   _____
3. you press this switch / light turns on
   _____
4. you add five and five / get ten
   _____
5. you feel sick / take some medicine
   _____

Lesson C

Real Conditionals: The First Conditional

If Clause (Simple Present)	Main Clause (*Will* for Future)
If you **leave** a message,	I **will call** you.
If you **don't study**,	you **won't** pass the test.

We use the first conditional to talk about a possible future action. Use the simple present in the *if* clause and *will* / *won't* to talk about the future action or result in the main clause.

With the first conditional, you can start with the *if* clause or the main clause. If you start with the *if* clause, use a comma between the clauses:

If you go now, you'll catch your train. = You'll catch your train if you go now.

C Complete the first conditional sentences with the correct form of the verbs in parentheses.

1. If you meet the bank manager, she _____'ll ask_____ (ask) you some questions.

2. If he _____ (be) late for work again, he'll lose his job.

3. You _____ (catch) the bus if you run.

4. I'll send you the document if you _____ (give) me your email address.

5. If it _____ (stop) raining, we'll go for a walk.

6. The police will stop her if she _____ (drive) faster than the speed limit.

7. If you _____ (not give) me any chocolate, I'll tell Mom and Dad!

8. If I'm tired tonight, I _____ (not go) out with my friends.

D Read the sentences with the zero conditional and the first conditional. Underline the correct verb form.

1. If you need some money, *go* / *will go* to the ATM.

2. Put on your coat if it *rains* / *will rain*.

3. If our friends come tonight, we *have* / *'ll have* a party.

4. If you don't pay me, I *didn't do* / *won't do* the work.

5. If you *press* / *will press* this button, the washing machine turns off.

6. We *meet* / *'ll meet* you at the airport if we have time tomorrow.

7. If you take a vacation next summer, where *do* / *will* you go?

8. I *ask* / *'ll ask* my parents for the money if the bank doesn't give me a loan.

Common Irregular Verbs

Base Form	Simple Past	Past Participle	Base Form	Simple Past	Past Participle
begin	began	begun	make	made	made
break	broke	broken	meet	met	met
bring	brought	brought	pay	paid	paid
buy	bought	bought	put	put	put
come	came	come	read	read	read
do	did	done	ride	rode	ridden
drink	drank	drunk	run	ran	run
drive	drove	driven	say	said	said
eat	ate	eaten	see	saw	seen
feel	felt	felt	send	sent	sent
get	got	gotten	sit	sat	sat
give	gave	given	sleep	slept	slept
go	went	gone	speak	spoke	spoken
have	had	had	swim	swam	swum
hear	heard	heard	take	took	taken
hurt	hurt	hurt	tell	told	told
know	knew	known	think	thought	thought
leave	left	left	throw	threw	thrown
let	let	let	understand	understood	understood
lose	lost	lost	write	wrote	written

Credits